T0199117

The Bills Keep Coming, the Grass Keeps Growing

The Bills Keep Coming, the Grass Keeps Growing

Survivor of a Suicide Gets on with Life

SANDI LATIMER

THE BILLS KEEP COMING, THE GRASS KEEPS GROWING
SURVIVOR OF A SUICIDE GETS ON WITH LIFE

iUniverse books may be ordered through booksellers or by contacting:

iUniverse
1663 Liberty Drive
Bloomington, IN 47403
www.iuniverse.com
1-800-Authors (1-800-288-4677)

ISBN: 978-1-5320-6007-6 (sc)
ISBN: 978-1-5320-6006-9 (e)

Library of Congress Control Number: 2018912124

Print information available on the last page.

iUniverse rev. date: 12/14/2018

Contents

Books Published by iUniverse

Poodle Mistress: The Autobiographical Story of Life with Nine Toy Poodles
Sandi Latimer

Newsroom Buddies: A Working Friendship at United Press International
Sandi Latimer and John Kady

Book Published by Gatekeeper Press

Bunny Bob: The Bumbling Easter Bunny
Sandi Latimer

Chapter 1

I'm a Survivor

The quarterback dropped back, looked downfield for a receiver, and unleashed a spiraling pass that a teammate caught. The teammate then raced down the sideline and into the end zone.

The home-team fans were cheering, me among them. I jumped up and down on the aluminum stands, yelling, "Go, kid, go!" The home team, Westland, my school in a four-high-school district, usually won just one game a year. But this year, the team was well on its way to a third straight win. I go to a football game every Friday night, dividing my support among area teams. The Westland game was the one I had chosen to go to that night.

I was happy, excited for these kids I didn't know. They deserved all the support they could get. Even though I was cheering, tears were flowing down my cheeks.

I was going to go home to an empty house—no one to replay the game for. I wouldn't hear "Did we win?" the moment the front door was opened. And I couldn't make a fist with my right hand, jab my right elbow into my rib cage, and yell, "Yes!"

I'm a widow now, and life *ain't* what it used to be.

A few years back—2009, to be exact—forty-five people were laid off from the *Columbus Dispatch*, including all the sports clerks, of which I had been one for eleven years. I was now free on Friday nights to go to high school football and basketball games, rather than collect scores and stats. My husband, Red, whom I'd married in the spring of 1974, decided to go with me. The first game he wanted to go to was at a school in our district that had an outstanding band. We stayed for the entire game to cheer on the team after many of the fans had left after halftime. The next week he wanted to go to another game in our district because it was the newest high school and he wanted to know where it was.

That's all he could take. His backaches made it difficult for him to sit for long periods of time on the hard bleacher seats.

"You go and tell me all about it when you get home," he said. And when I got home each Friday night, the phrase "Did we win?" rang out even before I had my feet in the door. If I had taken pictures at the basketball games, he had to see them right away. He laughed hard when I showed him the photo of a high school fan dressed in black slacks and a black-and-white-striped referee shirt, wearing dark glasses and carrying a white cane.

I hated to leave him, now that he had been retired for several years and I had some free time on my hands, but he insisted I go out and enjoy myself. He was so full of questions when I returned.

If he wasn't waiting for me in the living area, he was down in the basement, where he had created a man cave—a place where he could sleep during the day when he was working third shift, watch TV programs I didn't like, or ride his bicycle on a trainer.

My tears were frequent and often came unexpectedly after he died. My voice cracked as I talked about the man with whom I had done many exciting things during the last forty years—things like his trying to teach me to fly, or going on picnics with our dogs on that warm day in February, or going to nearby lakes so he could ride his WaveRunner. When my voice did crack, I'd have to stop talking, take a deep breath, and resume in my normal voice.

I tried to do things the way he did them or the way he'd want them done. Some things I just couldn't do. I couldn't start the pull-start lawn mower. Fortunately I had help from neighbors in mowing the yard. I can change light bulbs, but when the burned-out bulb is too high for me to reach and not in a safe place for me to use a step stool, I need help.

My friend Jean, who has lost two husbands, told me that I was just going to have to break down and ask people to help me. For someone who rarely had to ask for help, I found that hard to do.

I did a lot of things the best way I knew how, especially renewing Red's automobile license plates a couple of months after he died. The titles were with the attorney who was helping me work on the estate. I couldn't sign to renew Red's plates in person, so I did the next best thing—I renewed them online.

Next year will be different, I told myself.

Oh yes, the next year *was* different. The estate had been settled, and I was able to transfer ownership of Red's SUV to me. I wanted to keep it. I felt I deserved this vehicle in addition to my own. After transferring the vehicle at the automobile title place, I went next door to the Bureau of Motor Vehicles to renew the plates for both the SUV and my car.

When I told the young woman at the counter I had just transferred the vehicle into my name and I wanted to keep the same plates, she asked whom I had transferred it from.

"My late husband," I said.

"I'll need his signature," she said.

"Honey, what part of 'late husband' do you not understand?" I asked, opening the folded piece of paper I always carried when I was doing work involving Red and the estate. "Here is a copy of the death certificate."

"Can he come in and sign it?" she asked.

"Honey, he's dead. Six feet under." I put it as politely as possible.

"Can he write a letter?" was her next question.

In my sweet little playground voice, I asked, "Can we have some help over here?"

The young woman, who looked to be a high school student working for the summer, walked back to get either a supervisor or the owner of the Bureau of Motor Vehicles. A woman accompanied her back to the counter, looked at the death certificate, and asked me, "Are you the surviving spouse?"

"Yes," I said.

The woman said, "She gets to keep her plates," and handed me back the death certificate.

I handed over a check for the two transactions and walked out of the building shaking my head.

The next time I went to the cemetery, I told Red of that conversation and asked that before he turned to dust, could he write me a letter.

Oh yes, life is different. I think of Red every day, something he'd say or do. I've made some new friends and found help from my new friends in a group no one wants to join but is glad to be present for. My support group. Members give me moral support, and I look forward to our weekly gatherings. But we all are living with one thought in mind—our loved ones chose to end their lives.

You see, not only am I a widow, but also I'm a survivor—a survivor of a suicide. I haven't talked about it much to anyone outside the family, except at support group. I fear the stigma that suicide carries within the community. But looking back at the couple of weeks leading up to June 9, 2014, I understand—or at least I think I do—what led Red to make that decision.

Chapter 2

You Don't Know What Pain Is

When I met Red in 1973, he was just getting back to work in the aviation section of the Ohio Highway Patrol, where he was a pilot. He had been off work for quite a while with a back injury, which he thought could have been exacerbated by a couple of rear-ending car crashes early in his career. He had had surgery to fuse a couple of discs in his lower back in the spring, and by late July he'd returned to work.

That's when I met him. And we were married in the spring of 1974. Two years later he retired and found work in security with a bank.

By 1978, scar tissue formed, but before the surgeon could operate, Red's sciatica nerve was pinched. Red was left with no feeling down the outer side of his right leg and would experience occasional shocks in what he called his bad leg. The pinched nerve also left him with a slight limp. He did a lot to disguise it. He had walked and climbed stairs and, since 2000, had ridden a bicycle daily at home and with his bike-riding friends every Wednesday. In the last few years, he had been riding a recumbent trike on those weekly rides.

Over time, he had cut down on eating. I figured it was normal with aging. After all, he was in his mideighties. He'd also lost a couple of inches in height from the six-foot-one figure he listed on papers when we were married forty years earlier. But then, people do lose height as they age.

As for his eating: "I'll eat when I'm hungry," Red said.

That sounded good to me. He'd often tell me what and when he wanted to eat. Several months earlier he told me he had to put a new hole in his belt. And he held up his belt to show me the new hole.

Red had also been seeing a pain doctor but complained so often about the other patients—their hygiene, their appearance. Then he started complaining that the injections he was getting weren't doing him any good.

"I'm not going back," he said.

"No sense spending money on something that doesn't work," I said.

In the spring of 2014, he began getting shocks in both legs.

Around Memorial Day he was hardly eating anything. In early June he wasn't eating at all, and I reverted to an old standby.

"When you say you don't feel good, you usually can get some tomato soup down," I suggested. Red agreed to it. But after sipping a couple of spoonfuls of it, he complained.

"It's no good. You ruined it!"

"I didn't do anything different," I said.

"It's too rich," Red said.

I was starting to get to my wits' end, but I couldn't let him see it. After all we had been through with each other—his back surgeries, his motorcycle crash, and his hernia surgeries, and my cancer and chemotherapy, my myocardial infarction and quadruple bypass, my congestive heart failure and fluid in the lungs, and the insertion of a defibrillator pacemaker—I figured we were entering another chapter in our medical history.

The next morning I suggested scrambled eggs and toast. Red agreed to two eggs and one piece of toast. I let him eat from a TV tray at his leather recliner rather than serve him at the table.

"That tasted good," he said in a childlike voice. "Can I have another piece of toast?"

I felt as though I was making headway. He'd eat scrambled eggs and toast. I'd fix what I wanted to eat. My kitchen seemed like a restaurant.

Sunday evening, June 8, I made a bowl of instant vanilla pudding.

Red was sleeping in his man cave, that special room he'd created in the basement so he could sleep during the day. When he worked third shift at the bank, he had difficulties sleeping during the day. He bought dark blinds for our bedroom windows. That didn't work. He put carpet scraps over those windows. That didn't work either.

As a last resort, he put up plywood paneling to block off one part of the basement and created a room without windows or heat. At last he could sleep during the day when I was working. For much of our married life we worked different shifts.

He even jury-rigged a desk lamp on the wall to provide a handy light over the bed. He was using the bed frame and headboard that my father had bought me for Christmas when I was in the eighth grade. He had TVs in there. He put a bicycle on a trainer, and he'd watch *The Young and the Restless* while riding his bike. It made me happy because he was getting his exercise and not bothering me with a TV program I didn't like.

On Monday, June 9, I got up early and went through my regular routine—shower, blow-dry my hair, read the paper before using the curling iron on my short graying hair. I probably made some noise, although I tried to be quiet as I got ready to go to my volunteer shift at HandsOn Central Ohio, where for more than a dozen years I had answered phones every Monday to assign callers to food pantries.

I hesitated that day. Red hadn't been feeling well for the past ten days or so. *Should I stay home and take care of him?*

But I carried through with my routine. I didn't want to wake him to say I was leaving. I knew what he'd say: *Why did you wake me? You know I don't feel good. I don't want to be bothered when I don't feel good.* I didn't want that on my mind.

So I didn't wake him. I figured he'd hear the garage door as it went up and then down.

A little after nine o'clock or so, I got this funny feeling at HandsOn. My fingers seemed to contract, and I felt my rings would fall off. I hadn't been able to get my rings off for a little over a year. I think my fingers were swelling from the effects of arthritis.

That strange feeling lasted only an instant. I continued with my phone call and forgot about that strange feeling.

I finished my shift at noon, stopped to chat with a couple of friends on my way out the building, and headed for home.

When I arrived home at one o'clock, something didn't feel right. As I walked to the bathroom, I thought, *It's awful quiet in here. Red should be watching* The Young and the Restless. *Maybe he's recording it and sleeping. Maybe he's watching it and muted the commercials.* He did that a lot. I knew he wouldn't be riding his bike, because Saturday when I'd stopped by his room I found him standing beside the bike. "It just isn't working," he'd said.

Rubbing lotion into my hands, I started down the steps—seven from the living room to the front door and landing, seven more to the basement. With a couple of steps to go, I smelled something unusual. I couldn't remember smelling anything like that before. It seemed to come from Red's room on the other side of the stairs.

Without turning on a light in the main part of the basement, I stepped into his room and, with my right hand, nudged his upper right arm as if to wake him. Red's arm felt like an I beam. It was stiff. I struggled to try to turn on the light above the bed, but I never got it on.

My heart was racing, and I swear I stopped breathing. I didn't want to believe what immediately ran through my mind. I reached over with the back of my left hand to feel his cheek. That's when I felt it.

What I felt was wood. I knew what it was and what had happened.

"Oh no," I gasped.

What I'd felt was the wooden handle of a handgun, one of his two Ohio Highway Patrol commemorative guns. One was from the patrol's fortieth anniversary, and the other was from the fiftieth anniversary. Neither had been shot before. Now one of them had.

He had shot himself. He was dead. He was turning cold and stiff.

I didn't panic, scream, or go into hysterics. If I were to scream, no one would hear me from the basement. I couldn't go into hysterics in front of my neighbors because they held me in such high esteem. After all, Red was dead; he was cold, and maybe rigor mortis was beginning to set in. There was nothing I could do for him.

Chapter 3

What Do I Do First?

I don't know how long I stayed in that darkened room. I don't know what I did. But when I came out, I looked down at my hands and saw that the gun was lying on them. I shovel-pitched it onto the cloth-covered reclining chair in the main part of the basement.

I'm a widow was the first thought that crossed my mind. I had enough wits about me to reach in the pocket of my slacks for my cell phone and call 911.

Red had explained to me several years earlier that when a death occurs at home, one should call the sheriff or the police, depending upon the jurisdiction. He had explained that to me when the woman across the street died in her sleep and was found later that day by her sister.

I climbed the steps as the phone was ringing at the 911 call center. I knew I had to be calm and that I should speak slowly so I could tell the operator which units to send. We live in a township a few streets outside the city limits. We are served by the sheriff's office and the township fire department and its EMS unit. Living on a border can be confusing. And if the caller is hysterical, it could mean the wrong unit would be sent.

I identified myself to the operator and gave her the address.

"I just got home and found my husband had shot himself," I said in a shaky voice. "I'm sorry, but I touched the gun."

The operator was calm and worked to keep me calm, repeating my address to make sure she had the proper people on the way.

"Where are you now?" she asked.

"I'm sitting on the steps leading to the living room," I said. And looking at my free hand, I added, "I'm shaking like an aspen."

She told me to stay where I was and said that she'd remain on the line with me until help arrived.

I don't know if we talked or, if we did, what was said. I knew I didn't want to come across as that screaming, wailing surviving family member I see on TV news.

"Here comes someone now," I said as I saw a sheriff's cruiser pull up. And then the emergency squad arrived. We hung up. I let the first responders in and guided them downstairs.

They wouldn't let me stay downstairs. I had to go upstairs.

I sat in my leather reclining chair. On the couch beside me sat the sheriff's department's chaplain. The first call he made was to the highway patrol to advise them a retiree had died. I don't remember telling him Red had been a highway patrol officer.

"By his own hand," I heard him say. I gulped. *Did he have to say that?*

Firefighters and paramedics lined up on the stairs, blocking my view. One of them said he delivered newspapers when he was a boy and we were one of his customers. Workers brought Red's body up the stairs. He was in a body bag—a white one, not a black one as seen on TV shows. I think I was in shock and couldn't cry. I wanted to go to him, to help him, but I couldn't get out of my chair. It was as if I were glued to the chair.

I had to notify the family. I called my nephew, my late brother's son Gavin who works downtown.

"I lost Red this morning," I said, trying to keep from crying.

"Oh!" he said as if he, too, were in shock. "I'm sorry."

He assured me he would be out after work.

Now Red's family. Suddenly I realized I didn't have phone numbers for them. I had his younger daughter Marlene's address handy, but I didn't have phone numbers for her or her older sister, Marsha. I figured the numbers were in his cell phone, but I wasn't sure how to retrieve them. Our cell phones were different because we got them at different times and were on different programs. *Where is his phone?*

"Where's his cell phone?" I shouted.

A sheriff's deputy told someone to get his phone. Fortunately the body hadn't been taken away and the cell phone was with the body. Sometimes cell phones can be used to track the last minutes or hours of a deceased person's life. Someone went out and got the phone for me.

I played around with buttons until I found what I needed. I put a call in to Marsha, but instead I got her husband Scott. Marsha called me back a while later.

Meanwhile, all that was running through my mind was *Will I have to take a lie detector test?* Red's second wife, Joyce, had taken her life because she couldn't stand the pain of cystic fibrosis. Red had to take a lie detector test as part of the investigation into his wife's death.

Did they think he had anything to do with her death? He found her dead when he came home from work, just like I found Red's body when I came home.

"We didn't find a note," said one of the sheriff's deputies, coming up from the basement.

"No need. I know why. He couldn't stand the pain," I said.

The only response I got from the deputy was "There was another gun downstairs. How many are there in the house?"

I couldn't answer then, and I can't answer *now.*

"He's law enforcement," another deputy said. "He's probably got several."

It wasn't long until Gavin arrived. His ever-present grin and happy voice weren't there. He sat where the chaplain had sat. He looked very solemn.

"You're all I have left now," I said.

He nodded. "I know."

His sister, Shannon, my niece, is an elementary school teacher in Florida. My father, my stepfather, my mother, my brother, and Gavin and Shannon's mother have all passed away.

Red's daughters and their families live along Lake Erie. He also has nieces and nephews living in various parts of the country.

I can't remember if, as people began leaving, I thanked them for their kindness.

After the last person left, I noticed a small white bowl on the TV tray by the side of Red's leather recliner. He had been up and eaten some pudding for breakfast. I felt so embarrassed that it sat there all afternoon while people were coming and going, but I hadn't seen it until late that afternoon.

That's when my neighbor BJ came over. I was glad to see her. She's the one who called on Red to perform so many tasks since she lived alone. He and I would both go over to do the job she needed done. Red wouldn't go over by himself because he was concerned about what the neighbors would think if they saw him going over there alone so many times.

I made a decision right there: I wasn't going to reveal the cause of death. Personally I wasn't ready to talk about it. I had a few questions in my own mind. I knew the who, the what, the when, the where, the why, and the how. I needed to go deeper into the why. *Oh dear, my journalism traits are kicking in.*

BJ and I made small talk, tried to laugh at a few light times. I had assured everyone all day I was fine, that I was going to be fine, that I would eat something and get some rest. "Yes, I'll call if I need anything."

And then I was alone. Really alone. The man I had loved and had spent more than half my life with was gone. He wasn't coming home. I had entered a new stage of life. "I'm a widow," I whined.

Chapter 4

Decisions, Decisions, Decisions

I had met Red in one of the strangest ways—at least to me it was strange.

I was working the night broadcast desk at United Press International in Columbus, Ohio, and was looking for stories to freshen my report. I put in a call to the highway patrol's communications center. I got a new voice. It was Red filling in.

"We get off at the same time," I said, a little brazen for me, as I invited him for a late night cup of coffee.

He asked for a rain check, saying he had to fly in the morning. I figured I'd never hear from him, figuring he was married. Was I surprised the next afternoon when he called and wanted to know if I wanted to cash in on that rain check.

I was in no way ready to meet anyone. I was wearing a sleeveless dress and dirty white sandals. My legs were in bad need of a shave. I suggested a lounge not far from where I lived. When I got there, I saw a red-haired man in a shirt, tie, and red sport coat standing in front of a red car.

I learned that night about his family, both two-legged and four-legged. He was raising two toy poodles, one just three months old. I had to meet them. That little one climbed up my leg and adopted me the day I went to meet the dogs. I always said it was a new twist on having to get married.

What a life Red had led. He played basketball in high school, on a gym floor we call "a postage stamp" today. He graduated in 1946 at a time when the men were returning home from World War II and getting their old jobs back. He was a few weeks shy of his eighteenth birthday when he persuaded his mother to sign for him to enter the US Army. He celebrated that milestone birthday learning to drive a tank at Fort Knox.

At that time he had to serve just eighteen months, and fourteen of them he spent in Korea in the Army of Occupation. He didn't like Korea and never ate rice or pork after that. He didn't like how rice was grown, and he'd gotten food poisoning on poorly cooked pork.

Upon discharge from the army, he returned home to northwest Ohio, bought an Indian motorcycle, and rode to Kansas City to enroll in plumbing school.

After that, he bided his time as an apprentice electrician until he could get on the Ohio Highway Patrol, which he joined on December 1, 1951.

His first marriage, which produced the two daughters, didn't last long. The second marriage ended in his wife's death, leaving him with two poodles. He kept one and gave the other to friends.

He was always an outdoorsman. His idea of camping was throwing an air mattress in the back of a station wagon. He'd had a boat and learned to water ski. He rode a bicycle as well as the motorcycle. When the state of Ohio put into effect in July 1968 a motorcycle endorsement on the back of an operator's license, he was the one who approved the maneuverability course.

Red also liked flying, taking after a brother who flew during World War II. He used his overtime pay from the 1970 campus riots at The Ohio State University to take flying lessons. And with the pilot's license, he needed a plane, so he bought a Beechcraft Bonanza. But he sold that when he transferred to the aviation section.

A few years later, the patrol was able to get new planes, and I was able to purchase one that was traded in. That sort of satisfied my love of flying, although I could take off and fly, but never learned to land. I got down so far but would pull up, and then Red would have to take over and get us down. I was afraid the propeller would get stuck in the ground or hit the runway and flip us.

Not many small airports have restaurants or attractions. If we did go to an airport without a restaurant, we'd have to have ground transportation to take us somewhere. Our little folding bikes couldn't handle our transportation needs.

"I want a motor home," Red said one night.

"What's a motor home?" I asked. A few weeks later one was sitting in front of the house. As I was loading the motor home for camping trips, Red was looking for a buyer for the airplane.

He still loved the water, so he bought a WaveRunner. I'm not a water person. I'd go to the water's edge, send him off, then go sit under a tree and read until he was ready to come in.

By 2000 we lost our last dog and decided it was time to do things for ourselves. Red went bike riding; I went walking. And we shared our experiences. "Where'd you go? What did you see? Did you get any pictures?"

Now I was taking deep breaths and pacing the floor until I thought I'd wear a path in the carpet. *Have I eaten? I don't know. Have I slept? No.* One thing I had to do was get the obituary typed.

For a long time, Red and I had talked about writing our obituaries so we'd have them when the time came. This started a few years earlier when he was reading the obituary page and laughing.

"What's so funny?" I said as I leaned over his shoulder that morning.

He pointed to the obituary of a World War II veteran who was, as Red pointed out, "a parrot trooper." We both had a good laugh and then straightened up.

"Well, if that's the way you want to be remembered," I said.

"Maybe we'd better write our obituaries ourselves, and then we'll know they are done right," he said.

We dragged our feet. He nagged me to get started on them.

Finally I wrote something and gave it to him. Being a longtime reporter, I look at an obituary as a news story. He saw an obituary as something that is provided to the newspaper by the funeral home. To me that is a death notice.

"Make the changes, and I'll type it up," I said.

Several days later he handed me the handwritten copy on a lined white legal pad.

"Are you satisfied with it?" I asked.

He said, "Yes."

On June 9, 2014, it was still lying on the dining room table.

I opened my laptop computer, but it wouldn't turn on.

"This is a fine thing," I said out loud. "First my husband dies, then my computer." I got Red's laptop but I was having trouble with it too. I couldn't move the cursor. Fortunately I could still use the desktop model in my catchall room. I could type the obituary and save it to a flash drive to take to the funeral home.

It was the wee hours of the morning, and I was wearing my flip-flops. My feet got cold.

If I'm cold, he's cold, I thought. I started crying, the first time I'd shed tears since I found him more than twelve hours earlier.

I walked out into the kitchen to get a drink of water. I glanced at the clock on the microwave oven: 5:28. Another waterfall of tears.

When Red entered the highway patrol, he was assigned a unit number: 528. That number popped up so much in our lives. And now here it was in death.

I lay down, but there was no way I could sleep. I got up and took a shower and tried to do something with my hair. I had to go to the funeral home and the cemetery. Or was it the other way around?

The answer to the question of what cemetery to use was easy. I had worked part time for eleven years for Green Lawn Cemetery, the second-largest cemetery in Ohio. I was the volunteer coordinator, a rare position in cemeteries. I had retired in January of that year.

I figured I had to go to the cemetery first and then the funeral home. That way I could tell the funeral director about the services and which cemetery I had chosen.

One day Red had told me which funeral home he preferred. I knew someone at that funeral home. It would be easy to work with someone I knew. I discovered that my task of handling the arrangements wasn't easy.

I made the calls early in the business day to set up appointments.

"Is my employee discount still in effect?" I asked Jack, the general manager of the cemetery. I tried to keep a stiff upper lip so I wouldn't break down. "I need it." And I started to cry.

"He was a veteran, wasn't he?" Jack asked. "Bring his military papers with you."

That was easy. I knew where those papers were, even if I didn't know what a DD-214 (discharge paper) looked like. Red had a big box in his catchall room that contained envelopes marked with the contents. One was marked "Military Papers."

My assigned family service adviser at the cemetery, Jeff, told me that a new section had been opened for military members and their spouses. In many cemeteries, veterans are buried in a section according to war or time served and the spouse would have to be buried elsewhere. I was happy that this section was being developed. I chose it.

"The first open lot," I said.

Since Red was a veteran, the Veterans Administration would be paying for his plot and his marker. I would have to pay for my plot next to him on that lot and the other half of the marker. Our lot is in direct line with an American flag, one of seven flags that outline that section.

My meeting at the funeral home went rather well because I knew Bob, the person assigned to me that afternoon.

As Bob and I walked through the casket room, I couldn't help but remember—and had to share the memory—the time my brother, only six years old at the time, came up missing the day we were picking out our grandfather's casket. We found him lying in a casket.

"I just wanted to know how Grandpa would feel," he'd said.

I found myself fingering the lining of a beautiful wooden casket. Red wanted wood. I chose the brand of vault my father had hauled in my preteen years.

Bob said he would take care of notifying the Social Security Administration. That would stop Red's Social Security checks.

"Was he a registered voter?" he asked, and I assured him he was. "I'll notify the Board of Elections."

Within minutes of getting home after taking care of these two tasks, I heard the phone as it started ringing.

BJ called. "Are you eating?"

Then my friend Pat called, trying to find out what I had planned for the funeral. "I can't come up with a preacher," I confided.

"You can use mine," she said.

"No, Pat. I appreciate your offer, but I don't know your pastor. I was married to Red for forty years, and I know what he needs."

I didn't want someone who didn't know either of us to stand up there at the casket, read some scripture, lead the mourners in the Lord's Prayer, and read the obituary from the newspaper. I especially didn't want the obituary or death notice read, because people who at the service would have already read it.

I went back and forth all afternoon with these two concerned women. And in the meantime I was trying to figure out how to handle the service.

Somewhere I found time to squeeze in a call to our attorney. He advised me what financial papers to gather so he could begin to work on the estate—a listing of Red's assets and what he owed. I'd need checking, savings, and investment account information, automobile titles, and proof of ownership of other large items that would be included in the estate. I also needed birth certificates, marriage license, and marriage certificate. Eventually I'd have to add the death certificate.

One of the first things I did was check Red's work area in the back room. I knew that June was a crucial period—property taxes had to be paid. The checkbook was out. I opened it to the check register. The property taxes had been paid, as had his school alumni dues. And a check had been written to Red's granddaughter Laura as her high school graduation gift.

I was astounded when I found a check that represented a life insurance policy Red and I had discussed every year.

"It's for you," he would say when the premium notice came due.

"If you want me to pay it, give it to me and I'll pay it," I would reply.

Here was the check, made out to him and dated just a couple of days prior in the amount of some pocket change less than the face value of the policy.

Then came the call from the coroner's office: Did I want an autopsy? To my surprise, the first words out of my mouth were "What is the cost?"

Since there was no charge, I thought I'd go for it. Of course, I knew how Red died, but I wanted to know if there was an underlying cause other than the pain he was suffering. He had only recently been to the urologist and stopped going to the pain clinic "because they aren't doing anything to help me."

Had the urologist found something he couldn't talk with me about? He always prided himself on the fact that no one in his family had cancer.

I had asked the probing questions and had gotten a sharp, crisp "No!" *Was he trying to tell me something?*

I had tried to encourage Red to go see his personal physician, but he'd said, "It's a pain filling out forms every time I go." I tried to explain that what he put on the form today was compared to what he had put down the last time and that if there was any change, the doctor could see it. But he'd stop me short.

"When did you get your MD degree?" he'd bark.

Somewhere during that afternoon I must have gotten my conversations with BJ and Pat mixed up because it was BJ who came through with the minister answer. Well, sort of.

Dion, who lived across the street and three doors up from BJ, rang my doorbell. BJ had explained he was certified to officiate at funerals and was studying to be able to preside over marriages. The answer to my problem.

Red and I had met Dion and his family the night they signed papers to buy the house across the street from us. They came over to introduce themselves because we were sitting in front of our garage. Red and Dion used to chat while mowing yards, while riding bikes.

"I don't want a 'We are gathered here today to mourn the loss' type of service," I told Dion. "I want it to be a celebration of life."

Another phone call came in, this one from the highway patrol. What did I need? I needed pallbearers, I admitted. I got them, and they doubled as the honor guard.

Wednesday would have been Red's bicycle riding day. I had to call the ride leader to let her know he had died so she could share the information with the other riders. Would she also be so kind as to say a few words?

Wednesday was also my writing group meeting day. I called one of the members to let her know I wouldn't be there. I also called a longtime friend with whom I had worked at the *Columbus Dispatch* in sports. He helped spread the word.

Tuesday was nearing an end. I had accomplished a lot, making and taking phone calls, working three phones—Red's cell phone, my cell phone, and the landline. Somewhere I even found time to slip over to the library to check in on email and Facebook. *I'll worry about the computers later.*

The autopsy would be completed Wednesday, and then the body would be released to the funeral home. The funeral would be Friday—Friday the thirteenth.

"I'm not superstitious," Red often said.

I lay down, but as soon as I hit the bed, I bounced right back up. *When is the last time I slept? When will I ever be able to close my eyes?*

The obituary appeared in Wednesday morning's newspaper. The phones started ringing again.

"Sandi, is that your husband's obituary? Honey, I am *so* sorry."

I heard such phrases of condolence and sympathy so often that I soon wondered what they meant.

Chapter 5

Taps Signifies the End

My life was beginning to become a blur. I had to figure out what to bury Red in and take those clothes to the funeral home. I also had to clean the house.

BJ brought over a meat-and-cheese tray that took up one shelf in my refrigerator.

"I don't need that," I protested.

"You have to eat," she countered. "And people will be coming in."

"There won't be anyone," I said. "His kids aren't coming in until Thursday. The funeral is Friday."

As I launched into the cleaning job on Wednesday, I picked up an armful of clothes to take downstairs to toss in the washer. I dumped the dirty clothes in the washbasin so my hands would be free to lift the lid of the washer. What a surprise awaited me. There were Red's bedclothes— sheets, pillowcases, and pajamas. His Monday-morning routine was to wash his bedclothes.

Now I got to wondering. *Was his decision planned ahead of time to be done when I wasn't home, or was it a spur-of-the-moment act?*

Many years earlier we had read a story of a woman with severe back pain who took her life with pills.

"I know how she must have felt," Red said at the time. "If I ever got to that point, I'd off myself too."

I never gave Red's statement another thought. Not until now. Was his pain that bad that he had to take his life? It was one question that I would ask myself over and over and know that I wouldn't get an answer. And it is just one of the many questions I have raised. His decision was something I knew I would have to live with. The list of things I would have to live with would keep growing.

Thursday I was outside on a step stool putting a container of corn on the spike of the squirrel feeder when an SUV stopped in front of the house. Out bounded grandson Chuck, who put the container on the spike for me.

"I'm sorry I wasn't much of a grandson," he said.

Red would have loved to have heard that statement. One part of the family was here—Chuck; his wife, Ashley, who was pregnant with their second child; and their two-year-old son, David. Also present was Red's older daughter, Marsha, and her husband, Scott. Daughter Marlene and her daughters, Caryn and Laura, would arrive the next morning. That one-hundred-plus-mile car trip would be too much for Marlene's husband, Mark, who had a bad back and neck himself.

Friday, the day of the funeral, dawned beautiful, as had every day that week. Red would have loved it. Good bike-riding weather. Good weather to work outside. He hadn't been able to use his zero-turn-radius riding mower, so he'd started the push mower so I could do the mowing. He didn't walk behind me telling me how to do it as he did once before.

Red had wanted an hour of viewing before a service, but I figured I might need more time, so I scheduled two hours. Viewing would begin at noon. I was up early. I was all dressed except for my shoes.

Where are they? I thought in a panic, down on my hands and knees going through the closet. *I can't let anyone see me this way.*

Suddenly I realized where my shoes were—the last place I had worn them, of course. I dug them out and sat in the middle of the bedroom floor looking at the mishmash of straps, sole, and heel. *How do I get them on? I wear dress shoes so infrequently that I don't know how to put them on.*

And of course that was when the doorbell rang. I had locked the front door before taking a shower. *They're here, dressed and ready to take me to the funeral home. And I'm standing here in my stocking feet holding my shoes by the heels.*

I figured how to slip my feet in between the straps. Then I staggered to the door to let the kids in. Unaccustomed as I am to wearing those shoes, I could hardly walk in them. *Am I that vain that I'll never let anyone know I found the shoes in a suitcase I had taken to a conference the previous summer?*

After the few hugs and "Are you okay?" questions, I climbed in the SUV with Marsha and her family. Marlene and her daughters had met them at the motel and were right behind them. As we pulled into the parking lot from one direction, my niece from Florida, driving for my nephew, pulled in from a side street.

The family was allowed to enter the viewing room. I needed someone with me, someone I could lean on. I reached around to get someone's hand. There was no one there but me beside the flag-draped casket. I stood there alone. All I could do was stare at Red and ask, "Why did you do it?" I was angry at him for his decision. And it has taken a long time for that anger to subside. Perhaps talking about it at my support group meetings has helped it wane.

I stepped aside to let others have their moment with Red, and then I pulled them all aside.

"He shot himself," I told them. "I didn't have a thing to do with it. He had been fighting shocks in both legs for about two weeks and couldn't take the pain any longer."

I looked at them. They seemed to be in shock. We all wiped tears away. I had the box of tissues close to me all day. That must be a big expense for the funeral home.

The highway patrol honor guard of four officers—two at the head of the casket and two at the foot—changed every fifteen minutes. Shannon was so impressed that she videoed the changing of the guard. One time little great-grandson David marched behind the officers.

People started arriving: a couple of former troopers, people I write for at the weekly newspaper, neighbors, my friends, Red's bicycle-riding companions. My walking friends, whom I'd only seen in shorts and jeans, were dressed up. I hardly recognized them. My Red Hat friends were there, as were my seniors friends, my writing group friends, former coworkers from United Press International where I was employed for some twenty-two years, the former general manager of the cemetery and her husband, camping club friends, and people from meetings that I cover for the weekly newspaper. Among the visitors were Red's nephew and his wife and his niece. I took them aside to explain what had happened. My friend from the *Dispatch* whom I'd known for ages took pictures.

"If there is anything we can do for you, just ask," said Rick, the fire chief from the neighboring township.

"You can bring my husband back," I said, nearly in tears.

"No can do, Sandi," he said, giving me a hug.

Dion opened the service and spoke of his and Red's chats as they mowed yards and took bike rides together. Bike leader Gail talked about how Red always arrived early, ready to help anyone and everyone. "Wednesdays won't be the same anymore," she concluded.

I told how Red and I learned from each other, how he taught me to prepare and eat Italian food, and how we did things together or else did things separately and shared our experiences. Surprisingly I stayed somewhat calm, not breaking down and not crying.

On the way to the cemetery, I sat in the front seat of Marsha's SUV holding a stuffed Snoopy. Years ago I had helped a group get this stuffed animal as a giveaway, picked it up, and delivered it to them. And I won it! Red liked it, although our poodles weren't too sure about it when I brought it home. One year for his birthday, Red said all he wanted was my Snoopy.

"Well, go get it," I said. "You know where it is."

"No, I want it for my birthday," he maintained. "You have to give it to me."

On his birthday, possession of Snoopy changed hands. Snoopy went with him everywhere. I can understand a child carrying a stuffed animal around, but an eighty-something-year-old man? Let him have his fun.

I clutched Snoopy a little tighter when a car tried to enter the freeway, but backed off when the patrol cruisers rolled by. Back in 1960 a car ran a stop sign and crossed the street between the hearse carrying my father's body to the cemetery and the car carrying the family. I thought we'd lose Mom at that time.

It was a traditional graveside service, including the folding of the flag and its presentation, and also the presentation of a patrol Stetson. The playing of *Taps* got to me. Red had earned it. He served eighteen months in the army, from August 1946 until January 1948. Fourteen months were spent in Korea in the Army of Occupation. To me, *Taps* means the end. Mom said she couldn't stand hearing it. She had three brothers who returned home from World War II, all of whom preceded her in death. And now when I hear *Taps* at patriotic observances, I almost cry.

I felt strange hosting both sides of the family at the house. I kept looking around for Red. I had an emptiness in my stomach. Gavin and Shannon didn't know much about Red's side of the family, and Red's side of the family didn't know much about them. So it was the first time both sides had been together.

I talked about Red's last days, even how he had carried my box of books in for me. He had asked if one of them was the book that John (my ex-boss) and I worked on. He hurt too much to read it. But his family would read it.

Shannon and Crystal from my side joined Ashley, Caryn, and Laura from Red's side around the dining room table and chatted. Others sat at the other end of the room. I tried to keep conversation going.

I politely—or as politely as I could—encouraged everyone to leave, offering the rationale of the long drives ahead of them, back to Sandusky and to Maumee near Toledo. I said I had a birthday party for an organization to attend.

I didn't have time to grieve. I couldn't stay home because I would cry. I went to the birthday party. Gavin invited me to his aunt's house for a cookout on Sunday. On Monday I was back to my normal schedule as though nothing had happened.

I tried to be my usual self, but deep down, I knew I wasn't. And I never would be again.

Chapter 6

Getting On with My Life

I'm a widow, but am I ready for this life? Might as well get on with it. I'm not one to sit around the house and cry. That was evident Friday night when I went to the birthday party for an organization. We had set up a book fair as part of the activities. Several people were betting on whether I would show.

"Of course she will," said the organizer. And when I arrived, she said, "See, told you she'd be here."

The hugs I got that Friday night and at Sunday's cookout with my nephew's mother's family really helped. A hug felt good.

"How are you getting along?" asked my nephew's wife, Crystal, when I arrived for the cookout.

"I'm finding this and that, but I didn't find *Life's Little Book of Instructions*," I started.

"You write it," Crystal advised.

"But I did find twenty-eight combs in a basket in his back room."

"He didn't have twenty-eight hairs on his head," she shrieked, waving her hands around her face.

I stayed calm, participated in conversations, stood tall, and didn't cry. I think I did a lot of crying the first few days. I was also beginning to get some sleep.

Monday morning I walked into HandsOn for my volunteer shift, and many people were surprised. Maybe they didn't know how to handle me. I don't think they expected to see me.

Am I crazy for returning to my normal schedule so soon? Am I supposed to lock myself in the house and cry? How am I supposed to act?

Sure, I had work to do right away. Not only was there work to be done around the house and for the newspaper, but also I had to gather things to take to the attorney to start work on the estate. I had canceled Red's credit card and explained that the final bill would be paid when the estate account was established. The woman on the other end of the phone understood that I sandwiched these necessities in between going to meetings for work, writing my news stories, and sending them to my editors.

I wasn't afraid to stay in my big house alone. The day after the funeral I called a friend to thank her for coming to the visitation. The first thing she asked me was, "When are you moving?"

No one said anything about moving. The house had been paid off many years ago. After all, I told myself Red would soon be home. *Wait a minute, where did that come from? That was forty years earlier.*

Two weekends after the burial there were fundraising fish-fry events in the area. I had rarely gone to them because Red didn't like fish. I could go now and not feel guilty. I asked BJ to go with me to the first one. Sometime that evening she asked the personal question: "Did he leave you well-off?" I told her I was fine. Later I told myself that if I were asked that question again, I'd say, *I was well-off before he left me.*

I really had no idea where I stood because we were still working on the estate. I had to go through two previous marriages, two stepdaughters, and some grandchildren, not to mention two employers and Red's investment accounts.

I'd already had a meeting with the Highway Patrol Retirees Association and found out how much I would be getting in widow's pension and from Red's life insurance. For a long time I operated in panic mode for fear the insurance wouldn't pay out because Red had taken his own life, but I got to keep the insurance payment. The patrol had already given me a check the day of the funeral to get me through until I could get some more money. That would be helpful for some people, but we were different.

At the time I met Red, I was thirty and had been on my own for seven years. He was forty-five. He told me I could keep the money I made and the money I had saved. We never merged our funds. When I found his checkbook, I realized our balances were about the same.

I used to joke that when he wanted to buy something and I told him to go ahead, he should leave some money for groceries.

Now I was beginning to look at figures I had only dreamed of and was wondering if I'd have to resurrect my high school math and relearn how to work with logarithms.

I hadn't yet been to the bank where Red had worked for sixteen years.

This wasn't the easiest time of my life. I was finding that out day by day, step by step. Had Mother failed when she was widowed and had not a clue as to what I would face? I was living in a different generation from my mother. And I knew my financial setup was quite different. *O Lord, give me help. May my mother rest in peace.*

Chapter 7

Did You Hear Me?

I was trying to establish some form of normalcy in my new life. I continued with my regular work, but I was adding all these things I had do for Red, as well as the many things he used to do around the house.

"Just make a list," advised Josh, the young man who lives across the street.

"I did, Josh," I said. "I have four pages of things I must do."

"Oh dear," he said, slapping his hand on his forehead.

I was trying to set aside time for me to have a few minutes of quiet. One of those moments was early in the morning, over breakfast while I read the paper. It was peaceful until the phone rang at eight o'clock.

A bill collector! The woman wanted to know when she could expect payment of Red's credit card bill. I explained that when I had called to cancel the card, I said I would pay the bill as soon as the estate account was set up. That wasn't good enough for this woman. She wanted the payment *now*!

To prevent any more of these early-morning calls, I paid the bill and made a notation that the bill had been paid in the column of the spreadsheet I was keeping for all the checks written. That way I'd know what check went for what when the attorney, his paralegal, and I were doing the final settlement of the estate. This was one of the many bills I would reimburse myself for.

While I was typing Red's obituary, I realized he hadn't said anything about his second career, that of working in security in a local bank. I typed it in.

After having met with the attorney and his paralegal, I started going through Red's personal effects and determining what I would need to work on the estate. I knew he had a wad of Barr dollar bills.

Joseph Barr was secretary of the Treasury in the waning days of the Lyndon Johnson administration, just long enough to sign his name for a run of one-dollar bills. Red had saved those bills he had come across. I thought he had 132 or so. *Where did that figure come from? I don't know.* I wanted to know if he put that money in our safe-deposit box or if he spent the bills after I thought I had convinced him they were worth as much as a dollar bill with someone else's signature on it.

Oh my gosh! Where's the safe-deposit box?

I knew the box had been in the large building where he worked in security. Then the boxes were moved to a small white-frame building on a side street within sight of where he worked. The big building now housed the state's Department of Rehabilitation and Corrections. That little white building was something else. The safe-deposit boxes had been moved to a branch office. I thought I knew which one, but I needed verification

Go to the bank where he did his business and see how they can help you in locating the safe-deposit box. I sat down with an officer. I tried to tell her that one of the bank's retired employees had passed away and that he and I had a safe-deposit box. I explained the history of the moves and wanted to know if she knew where those boxes were now. I just wanted to know if there was anything in ours that I would need to add to the estate. I also wanted to close Red's accounts or at least put a hold on them so no action could take place.

The woman told me she couldn't do anything about the safe-deposit box unless I had a key. She seemed to be more focused on the safe-deposit box than on helping me through the process of what needed to be done when a retired employee of the bank died. *In all my nervousness and naiveté, did I forget to mention the person I was referring to is my now late husband and that the box is in both our names? I should have brought a copy of the obituary.*

A few days later a notice arrived in the mail stating that Red's pension for July had been deposited in an account I had tried to close.

Calm down. Regroup. Plan a new strategy.

Going back to the bank, I went in and talked to the same woman. I wanted to know why Red's pension had not been stopped, but she didn't have an answer to that question. I also had a key that to me looked like it belonged to a safe-deposit box. She looked it over and went to check on what I thought might be the location.

"The box isn't at this branch," she said.

I'd known that much going in. All I wanted was a location. And I didn't get any help with stopping deposits into a dead man's account. After all, Red had been retired for twenty-two years. The bank he worked for had been bought out. Perhaps these people didn't know much about former employees.

I mentioned something on my Facebook page about how stymied I was. I was getting responses that I should talk to an officer of the bank. Duh, whom do you think I was talking to?

I visited the bank a third time when Red's pension for August was deposited. Still no help on the location of the safe-deposit box, but I think the woman I spoke with both times understood my quandary about Red's pension going into a dead man's account. I still didn't get much response to my statement that he was a retired employee, even though I had his ID badge with me.

In the middle of August while I was in Fairborn for the Sweet Corn Festival, I was walking with Chris, a friend who was handling her mother's affairs. I explained my problem, and she suggested I go to the bank's website.

That I did when I got home that Saturday afternoon. I found a path to their Facebook page and left a message indicating my attempts to find the location of the safe-deposit box. I also was able to send a similar email message to a nameless person at an email address that would land in someone's email box. In the message I mentioned a retired bank employee had passed away and that the bank was putting pension money into a dead man's account for which I thought I had stopped transactions.

Lo and behold, I got an immediate response to the Facebook message. A young woman and I made telephone contact, and she was able to tell me where the box was located. The next business day I visited the branch that the nice young woman told me about. I found a lot of paperwork in the safe-deposit box that was vital, but there was no money or anything for the estate.

By Monday afternoon I had a toll-free number to call to get answers to the rest of my questions.

Thank you, Chris, my walking friend, for helping me along.

I called that phone number and found out I needed to send copies of my and Red's birth certificates, our marriage license and certificate, and his death certificate to an address in Charlotte, North Carolina.

The first of September I was driving to Greenville, South Carolina, for a conference, but I was stopping off in Asheville, North Carolina, to spend a couple of days with my longtime friend Jean. In my luggage I carried copies of the birth certificates, the marriage license, the marriage certificate, and Red's death certificate. I'd also brought a big envelope, stamps, and return-address stickers, just in case I had to send the documents again.

It was about this time that I was beginning to realize my birth certificate wasn't worth a hill of beans. It showed the name I was given when I was born seventy years earlier. Since then I had married and taken my husband's name. That's why I had to show my birth certificate, Red's birth certificate, the marriage license, and our marriage certificate just to prove I am Sandra Latimer.

I called that toll-free number in Orlando when I arrived in Greenville. I got ahold of the gentleman I had spoken with earlier. He assured me everything had arrived safely to him in Orlando, Florida, and was being processed. I could now enjoy my friends and the conference.

A while later I went back to the bank's website out of curiosity. There I found a tab "To Report a Death." They had revised their web page. I hope it helps someone in the future.

The pension payments to the account stopped. The next correspondence I got from the bank advised me that the three months' worth of pension checks deposited into my late husband's account would have to be returned. If I didn't pay back that amount by a given date, I would have to pay interest as a penalty.

The first check I wrote when I got the estate account set up was to the bank to cover those pension payments.

And soon my widow's benefits started coming monthly, retroactive to the date of Red's death. And then came the life insurance, although I had the same feelings I'd had earlier with the patrol's insurance. Would I get the insurance money even though Red had taken his own life? Both insurance policies were with the same company.

Chapter 8

Two Boxes of Cereal?

Once things calmed down somewhat, I realized I needed to go to the grocery store—and for more than milk and a head of lettuce.

I hadn't done much shopping of late. After Red retired in 1992, he discovered a lot of things around the house he liked to do. One of them was grocery shopping, for small trips. He'd come home apologizing that he couldn't find "scratch" and asking me what aisle it was in. For major shopping trips, we'd go together. He also liked to go to Sam's Club. He could handle the bulk items a lot better than I could.

Up and down the aisles of my neighborhood supermarket I went that day, putting items in the cart. *I need this, I want that.* Into the cart it went.

I got to the checkout counter and started putting items on the belt.

My God! It looks like I'm shopping for two. Oh well, I'll have plenty to put on the pantry shelves in the basement.

About the only thing that resembled shopping for one was the half gallon of milk. I never was much of a milk drinker, and a half gallon would last me quite a while since I used it mainly for cereal.

One item in my cart that day has now become a regular purchase: a bouquet of flowers. Several of the baskets of flowers from the funeral home were sent home with me rather than being left at the cemetery during the hot weather. I grew to love the fragrance wafting through the house. I had a lot of small vases and bud vases that had accumulated over the years with hospitalizations. I figured I might as well make use of them.

I also started making trips to Sam's Club. A dozen rolls of paper towels. A half dozen boxes of tissues. A big package of toilet paper. Two large boxes of cereal. Tomato soup, a dozen cans.

I even bought the same pastries Red bought in the big box. I was going to the cemetery every Sunday, and I'd take a pastry out of the freezer and stop somewhere for a cup of coffee. I'd sit in a lawn chair and have breakfast with Red.

At first I'd buy things he bought, thinking I was buying them for both of us. But as time went on and I realized it was just me, I still bought much the same way he did—or bought the same items and brands he did. Some items I didn't buy in quantity because either I didn't like them or didn't need that much.

When his Sam's Club membership expired—it had both our names on it—I got a membership in my name.

I was finally getting on with my life as a single person. *Or was I?*

One day about two and a half years after Red died, I was at Sam's Club, pushing the cart with list in hand. At the top of the list was cereal. As I got to the aisle with the cereal, I picked up a double box and put it in the cart. *Now I have to get my Cheerios at the other end of the aisle,* I thought and pushed the cart a few feet farther to pick up the double box of Cheerios. When I started to put my purchases on the conveyor belt at the checkout counter, I noticed I had a double box of Cinnamon Toast Crunch.

"That's Red's cereal. Why did I buy that?" I asked half aloud. For a long time I ate a bowl of cereal with half Cinnamon Toast Crunch and half Cheerios.

Now that the food was in the house, I discovered another problem. I later found out it is a problem a lot of people face. How do I cook for one?

I'd make a pie. Too much for me, so I'd share with BJ or take the rest to my support group.

I'd make vegetable lasagna, but it seemed I was eating it for three days, maybe four. I eventually would make a sizable amount of food to take to the seniors' potluck, and if I was lucky, I'd have leftovers for dinner that evening or the next day.

I thought I'd look back to how I had managed forty or so years before. But back then I didn't have a Sam's Club or other warehouse club to shop at. I didn't have a Crock-Pot or a microwave. Those were just becoming necessities in the kitchen when Red and I were married.

I'd make soup and freeze some of it. I learned to eat ham and beans with corn bread, even eating it a second day. As Red would say: "If it is good today, it'll taste better tomorrow." Oh how right he was!

I tried some frozen microwavable dishes. I didn't care for them.

One day at a meeting of volunteers as I was standing in line to go to the buffet, I overheard a woman say, "Mom is finding it difficult to cook for one now that Dad has died."

I guess I'm not the only one.

Chapter 9

Where Is Competence?

A few days after Red's passing, I finally figured out how to find phone numbers. We had different models of cell phones, different contracts. All I wanted was a phone to make and take calls. I felt a little intimidated, but I managed to weave my way through his phone. He had put in numbers not only of his family members but also of his bicycle friends and a lot of businesses he needed to call. He probably never thought I might need them too.

What a wealth of numbers I finally found! I knew that I had to copy many of those numbers somewhere before I turned off his service.

At first I didn't know where to put them. I didn't have an address book to put them in. Address books are almost a thing of the past with today's technology. But I did find a notebook I had won as a door prize at a writers' program. That would work for an address book.

It took a few days to copy the numbers. By then I had found all the numbers I would need on a sheet of paper hanging on the wall in Red's catchall room. I had never paid attention to what he crammed into that room, and he didn't pay attention to what I put in my room. That's how we used the two other bedrooms in the house.

By the time I was getting ready to go to the Carolinas, I had all I needed out of the phone and called the provider to terminate the service. I made a note of the date and the person I spoke with to terminate service.

I wanted service turned off September first, but I received a bill for September and then another in October. That note I had made of whom

I'd spoken with, on what date, and for what reason came in handy. I called the provider again and, as always, got a different person. I started to explain, and the woman said, "Yes, I can see you talked to that person on that date."

As I continued to tell her that I was still getting billed for that service, she was sympathetic. She erased one month's service and promised to shut off service as of the end of that current billing cycle and not charge me for it.

I did not get a bill in November 2014. *Good. This is all taken care of.*

Fast-forward to spring 2015 when I called a lawn care company to handle the weed situation in my yard. I was left with a storage shed full of equipment that I didn't know how to handle—especially the pump sprayer and a wheeled sprayer that hooked on to the riding lawn mower that was too large for me to handle. I had been trying to do the weed-killing job with a one-gallon flower-garden-type sprinkling can. Mix a little weed killer in a gallon of water and sprinkle the yard. Sprinkle a couple of dandelions, refill, and sprinkle a few more. What a long, tedious process.

That's when I called for help. Red had used this company but said he was dissatisfied with them and had canceled. I decided I'd try them, but I, too, soon became dissatisfied with the service. Once, when they called and said they were coming out on a specific date, I asked them to call me beforehand because I wanted to be there when they arrived.

On the specified date, the person arrived at my house.

"You were supposed to have called before you came out," I said.

"I did," the serviceman replied. "I left a message."

"I've had my cell phone in hand or in my pocket all day and it hasn't rung," I said. "What number did you call?"

He checked his records and rattled off my husband's number.

"That number belonged to my late husband. I requested it discontinued nine months ago," I said. "Your company has my cell phone and my landline numbers on record. Did they not update your information?"

I was beginning to get a headache.

Chapter 10

What Else Can Go Wrong?

One thing I heard from people after the initial shock of Red's death waned was "Don't make any major decisions for a year."

Some friends bemoaned the fact that they had used their spouse's insurance money or funds from the estate on a particular item they thought was nice and felt they needed but later wished they hadn't bought. Not me. I rarely purchase anything unless I really need it.

I decided I wasn't going to be like my mother either. My father died in 1960, on the last day of my junior year in high school. By the time I celebrated my seventeenth birthday three months later, Mother had bought a stereo system on which to play a record that she had had on order when Dad became ill. Then she bought a two-piece sectional couch and had the accompanying tables on order when she realized she didn't have room for them. Instead of recalling the order, she bought a house to put them in. And that is where we had my birthday party.

I wasn't going to be that extravagant. I am conservative and had been married to another conservative.

It wasn't long before things began to happen, things over which I had no control.

I nearly went into shock when the water bill arrived early in July. Red and I had always complained about paying an equal amount for water and sewer and then paying a surcharge to help those who couldn't pay their bills. But this bill was out of sight—nearly eleven hundred dollars for some eight thousand cubic feet of water.

I searched through past bills to find that our water bill was usually for around four hundred cubic feet. Either I had a leak or the meter had been read incorrectly.

I called the water office to ask about the bill.

"Did you fill a pool?" the woman asked. "Did you have family in?"

I figured the meter had been read wrong. Someone came out to reread the meter. He also installed a new meter. Fortunately there was no charge for this. This man agreed the meter had been read incorrectly. This new meter reads like the odometer on my car. I can keep an eye on how much water I'm using, and to determine the water bill, the meter is read from a passing vehicle. I got a new bill, a more reasonable one.

Next thing I knew, the smoke detector was beeping. I couldn't reach it to change the battery. I put recyclables in my car and delivered them to the recycle bins behind the fire department. Then I stopped in at the fire department and asked for someone to stop by and replace the battery in the smoke detector. The next day firefighters stopped by to change my dying battery.

In late July, I started working a twelve-day shift at the Ohio State Fair at an information booth, as I had been doing since 2009. I came home one afternoon with a funnel cake I had bought on the way to my car. I carried it carefully because it was on a paper plate with another as a lid. I took it in the house first and then turned around to go put the car in the garage. There stood Dion at the front door.

"You didn't see this," he said, pointing to the north side of my property.

I looked to where he was pointing. *How could I have missed it?* "Oh my gosh!" I gasped.

The chain-link fence separating my property from Steve's next door had been ripped out, stretched, and torn. From the looks of the tire tracks, it had happened moments before I got home.

"I saw the truck as it sped away, but I couldn't get a license plate," Dion explained. "I called the sheriff's office, but they said I couldn't do anything until the property owner came home."

A pickup truck had apparently come around the curve just north of my house and gone out of control, through Steve's yard, through my fence, stopping inches short of the gas meter. The driver then backed up. The fence must have become caught on the undercarriage, and that's when the truck tore out two fence posts, leaving one bent and lying in the middle of the street. Dion's son Marcus retrieved it. *How did I miss hitting the fence post on my way home?*

After I quit shaking and calmed down, I thought about Red's daily morning questions. When he'd come to breakfast, he always had three questions: How many people got shot overnight? Where is the overturned truck blocking a freeway ramp? Where is the car in the house? Those were usually the early-morning news stories. And now it was my house that almost made the news. I always thought the house was set far enough back that it was safe. I'm not so sure of that anymore.

Steve was not allowed to have a cell phone where he was working, so his phone was in his car. I called and left a message shortly before he got off work. By the time he rushed home, neighbors from the other side of me had gathered in the side yard. We surveyed the damage, including the ruts in the yards from the vehicle's wheels and the torn and stretched fence.

"If it had hit your gas meter and blown up your house, mine might have gone too," said Steve, putting his hand on my shoulder. "At least you're all right."

Yeah, I'm all right. What do I do now? What would Red do? He's not here. I have to do it.

Thank heaven for the big cardboard box where Red kept an envelope with paperwork for every major purchase. I quickly found information about our homeowners' insurance policy.

As soon as I get home from the fair tomorrow, I'll start calling around for estimates, I thought and added that task to the proper list of things to do. Not only was I keeping a list of things I paid for on Red's behalf, but also I was keeping separate lists of things I had to do for the estate and my work assignments and things I had to do around the house, even those as small as doing laundry or eating dinner.

I got two estimates for the fence—one that exceeded the deductible and one that seemed reasonable. The latter is the one I chose.

One afternoon the following week, I came home from an afternoon assignment and found four college-aged students in my yard at the opening in the fence.

The workers aren't supposed to be here until tomorrow, I thought as I put the car in the garage.

"We finished our last job early, so we figured we'd come out and get yours done," one of the young women said. "We'll be done here in a couple of hours."

They handed me an invoice and told me where to send the check. And with the yard cleaned up, they took off for their next job.

I was able to have the fence repaired for less than the deductible on the homeowners' insurance! *Dodged that bullet.*

Later that summer I began working on Red's project for the summer—taking up the asphalt driveway and replacing it with concrete. The driveway needed work before I fell into a pothole. I called the contractor whom Red wanted to do it and hoped it could be taken care of before the weather turned cold. I wasn't sure what it would cost, but I had a figure in mind. What the contractor quoted me was less than I had thought it would be.

One day as the work was being done, the contractor hooked up a hose to the outside spigot. A while later I went downstairs to do laundry and found water running from the wall toward the drain near the washer. *Now I know why Red hadn't used the front spigot for a while,* I thought as I raced up the stairs and out the door to have the workers shut off the water.

The water line going from the front spigot to the basement to the water meter had sprung a leak. *Is that why he had a plastic container on a popcorn tin?* The plastic container was filled and overflowing.

Why didn't he fix that? How long had it been that way? Surely he knew how to fix it since he went to plumbing school after he got out of the service. Oh well, another job that has to be done. Put that on a to-do list.

Fortunately I caught the leak in time. The water had run in a wide rivulet toward the drain. I swept the water toward the drain and looked for any damage. One box was in the way. It was damaged beyond saving, but the contents—family photos—had not gotten wet.

New fence partition. Driveway done. Now I had to change the filter in the furnace. *No problem,* I told myself. I had sat in the basement one day and talked to Red as he changed the filter. Not one of those flat rectangular things. This one had the pleats and combs.

I picked up the new filter from the furnace company.

"If you need help putting it in, bring it here and we'll help you," the customer service man said.

The hardest part was figuring out how to remove the filter frame from its slot at the side of the furnace. I worked on it, and forty-five minutes later I had the new filter installed! *Score one for me!*

Now I'm ready to settle in for the winter, I thought.

The Tuesday before Thanksgiving I had a few errands to take care of. I was planning to meet Red's niece and nephew and their families for dinner that Thursday at the Plaza, a small country restaurant near Mount Victory, where he grew up. I walked into the house in the middle of Tuesday afternoon and was greeted with the odor of an electrical burn.

Dropping everything, I raced through the house, sniffing, looking. I couldn't find any smoke or fire, but I did find a couple of places where the odor was stronger. Minutes later the smoke detector started going off. I grabbed my cell phone and called 911. Within minutes the fire department arrived.

These guys in full turnout gear were up in the attic area and all through the living area on the main floor. One was snooping in the basement. It seemed like forever before the one in the basement hollered, "I found it!"

The circuit board of the furnace had burned out. The firefighter had turned off the gas to the furnace.

"Better call a furnace repairman," he advised.

Again another trip to that box where the envelopes of paperwork were kept. I found the one with the information about the furnace. I asked the firefighters what all they had done. I wrote it all down and included their suggestions.

I called the furnace company quickly—fortunately it was before five in the evening. I was able to get a repairman to come out that night. He arrived around eight o'clock, looked it over, and gave me advice.

"You can have it repaired and still have a seventeen-year-old furnace," he started.

Was it that long ago that we bought that furnace?

Parts plus labor equals the cost of a new furnace?

He must have been reading my mind. Or I must have had a strange look on my face.

"I'll send a salesman out in the morning," he said.

Early the next morning a furnace salesman was sitting in my living room with flyers advertising furnaces. He also had schematic drawings of the house from the time seventeen years earlier when Red and I had bought that furnace.

I sat beside him, looking at the flyers and listening to what he was saying.

BTU. I've heard that phrase and associated it with heat, but that's about all I know. EnergyStar. I've seen that sticker on appliances and know it means energy efficient.

I don't know a thing about buying a furnace! went screaming through my head.

Sweetie! Where are you when I really need you? Help me, please!

I took the salesman's word and ordered a furnace. And I had just changed the filter a few weeks before.

"Let's see," the salesman began. "Tomorrow is Thanksgiving, and the next day is Friday, so no one is working."

He could see the little cube heater and the electric heater with oil in the fins that I had used for a couple of hours at a time when I was awake.

"No one is working Saturday or Sunday," he continued. "The earliest I can get you a new furnace is Monday."

I was counting on my fingers. *Almost a week without heat!* My neighbor BJ had called me as soon as the fire department had left the afternoon before, and when I told her my problem, she offered me a bed.

I made it through Tuesday night and Wednesday night.

I opened the cabinet doors under the sink in the kitchen and the bathroom to give the areas some heat from my little heaters. I did not run the heaters at night. It wasn't really cold, but if I had to go a week without heat and the temperature did drop, I might have to wrap pipes to protect them from freezing.

I can do that, I thought, speaking to Red. *It might not be the job you'd do. You're the one who went to plumbing school. I went into journalism.*

After a sumptuous Thanksgiving meal with Red's niece and nephew and their families, I returned to a cold house. Although I had had a good time, I was emotionally drained. Entering a cold house didn't help cheer me up. I was on the verge of tears. I stuffed a few things in a plastic bag to hold me for the night and crossed the street to a warm house.

"Why are you crying?" BJ asked.

Hey, I've lost my husband. I've just come back from dinner with his family. And I don't have heat in my house. Wouldn't you cry too?

I was at my house during the day and with BJ when it got dark. Monday afternoon, the installer finished the job by five o'clock. I wrote out the check.

Merry Christmas to me! I locked the door behind him and set the house alarm, the first thing that I had put on my to-purchase list after paying for the funeral.

Several people assured me that none of these expenses was a major decision. Any of these episodes could have happened when Red was alive or at any other time in my life. But for such things to happen during a period of heightened stress only made them seem so much worse.

And then I remembered a noontime program I'd attended when I worked at The Ohio State University Medical Center. The presenting doctor was talking about surgical procedures and said, "It may be minor to the surgeons, but anytime they cut on me, it's major."

To paraphrase that doctor whom I'd heard so long ago: Anytime they take my money, it's major.

Chapter 11

Working on the Estate

One of my calls I'd made in the hours after I found Red's body was to our attorney. He had the will, and he'd be able to advise me on some financial matters.

I followed his instructions of what to bring with me when I visited the office the week after the burial. I found a box and loaded it with the income tax records from the past couple of years. Also included were receipts of bills Red had paid so far that year, checkbook, and bankbooks. Anything I could find about investments went into the box. Also included was the insurance company check that was almost face value and a couple of other checks. Titles to the vehicles. Red's military papers. His and my birth certificates. Our marriage license and marriage certificate. His wallet. Money that I found among his belongings. I kept finding money in various places for a while.

I had a folder with a notepad in it, something I had received at a workshop. At last I had a reason to use it. I tossed that in the box the day I drove up to see the attorney. I wondered if I'd remember his face. It had been years since we'd had need of him.

The attorney, his paralegal, and I sat in a small conference room and went over everything I had brought. The paralegal was taking inventory. Some items I didn't need, but since I'd never done anything like this before, I'd brought whatever I thought I might need to set up the estate.

During our meetings, I also took notes of what I needed and the next steps I'd have to take.

We couldn't do much for the first thirty days because the will said I had to survive Red by that period or else everything would go to his older daughter. Red and I had written the wills early in our marriage, and we had done a lot of traveling together, both in an airplane and in motor homes. The will was written that way in case we were injured or killed in an accident. Had it been the other way around, everything would have gone to my mother or my brother. However, both had passed away by this time. *Oh dear, I must rewrite my will.*

And the paperwork I signed! I was wife number three. Red's first marriage had ended in divorce, and his second marriage ended in his wife's death. There were papers to be signed by his two daughters declaring that they wouldn't contest the will or try to lay claim to the house or any possessions.

I worried every time paperwork was sent to Sandusky. I shouldn't have had to worry, but one never knows. The daughters were good. They said they wouldn't contest the will. They said they would be cooperative. They signed the papers and sent them back. No problems. They were so nice about everything and told me later that they had their wills set up much the same as Red's and mine were. It sounded strange, but I had to realize Marsha was only ten years younger than I am. These young women were so nice to me during my rough times. I'm so glad to have them in my life.

By November, I was able to establish an estate account—all Red's active accounts were closed and funds transferred into one account. And I even had the checks to prove it. I could now pay his bills with checks from the "estate of Hugh M. Latimer Decd [deceased], Sandra L. Latimer Extr [executor]" and similarly signed by me.

Every time I saw BJ, it seemed she wanted to know how I was coming along with the estate.

"What do you mean, you don't have the estate settled?" she would ask. "We got Mom's settled right away."

"Well, you didn't have to go through two previous marriages, two daughters from a previous marriage, an employer who didn't understand for three months that one of its retired employees died," I said. *And I could go on and on.*

I'd get an email from the paralegal. Could I meet the attorney on a given day and time at the courthouse? My attorney and I would meet at probate court, on one of the high floors of a downtown building. I'd sign papers; we'd talk—about anything that came to mind. We talked about writing, about the new hall of justice across the street. At the end of the meeting I wandered across the street and walked through the lobby of that glass and steel building.

Then came the day the paralegal sent an email advising me the house was now in my name. I sat in the living room staring, where I don't know. *I'm a homeowner now,* I kept telling myself.

Ho-MOAN-ership is how a friend described it. It's more than living in a house and paying utilities, taxes, and insurance. It becomes *How do I get this done?* and *How do I get that done?* I needed a nail for a small job and didn't know where to find one in Red's workshop area. And trying to find one at Home Depot one street over was nearly as daunting.

Then I started receiving letters and phone calls from realtors and realty companies wanting to buy my house. Their letters started off, "Sorry about the loss of your loved one." And the next paragraph was "I want to buy your house."

I got so mad about these letters and the messages left on my voice mail that I returned the calls after normal business hours and left messages like, "Just because there's a transaction in probate court doesn't mean the house is for sale. I have to have a place to live."

Sometimes I'd write that note in the margins of the letter the realtor sent and return it to the sender.

I know at times what I wrote didn't sound good, but I was mad at their audacity. After all, this was and is my home where I'd lived for more than forty years. Furthermore, it was going to take forever to clean out my and Red's accumulations.

Meanwhile the bills kept coming. The paralegal had advised me to keep a ledger of the bills I paid. I had one checking account at this time—mine. I didn't yet have permission to sign checks on the estate account.

I paid Red's credit card bill, cell phone bill, and car bills. I paid my credit card bills, phone bill, and car bills. I paid the household bills. All of this came out of my checking account. My ledger contained a code—for Red's bills, for my bills, and for household bills. I also had one credit card that had a zero balance, and I kept it that way. That was for Red's special bills—service for his two cars, even renewing his license plates.

He died in June, and the license plates for both the 2002 Mercury Cougar and the 2010 Lincoln MKX had to be renewed in late August. The plates on my 2010 Ford Focus had to be renewed a month later. I was frantic. *What do I do?*

A day or two before the last day, hour, and minute (as Red was fond of saying), I decided to renew all three online. *After all, no one is going to know he isn't alive.*

His two went on that one credit card; my plates went on one of my other cards. For a long time I worried about whether I would get caught. Never happened.

It did seem that things were moving slowly. Paperwork between Columbus and Sandusky took time. And it took time to get onto the docket in the probate court.

I may have been able to avoid a lot of that probate court action if Red's bank accounts had listed me as beneficiary *and* if he had designated his accounts as payable on death—POD. That way I would have had access to his money immediately, if I would have needed it.

My accounts are all POD and have been for quite a while. Had anything happened to me, Red would have had access to those funds immediately since he was the beneficiary on the accounts. As soon as possible after Red died, I made a trip to the bank and changed the beneficiary on all my accounts. I even met with my financial adviser and made sure all the investment accounts were either POD or TOD (transferable on death) and the beneficiary was updated.

My niece and nephew are joint beneficiaries and should have little or no problem when I leave this world.

A little more than a year after we started this estate work, I was beginning to see the end.

I had a final meeting with the attorney and the paralegal. They explained how I was to close out the account.

The paralegal and I went over the ledger I had emailed her and totaled up Red's bills I'd paid—starting with the funeral. I was to write a check to myself and put that in my checking account.

"You're paying yourself for paying his bills," the paralegal explained.

"Okay," I said and wrote the check. This would go into my checking account.

Then the attorney presented me with his bill, and I wrote a check and presented it to him.

After those two checks cleared the bank, I was able to reconcile the account, write the final check to me, close out the account, and deposit the check in my account at my bank.

A little more than a year, and I was done with that chore. However, I had one more task to do.

I once asked Red if he had made any plans for his daughters, and he replied, "I'm leaving that up to you."

I had conferred with Marsha and Marlene about what they wanted or needed. They both said they were taken care of.

"Take care of yourself," they both told me. I still felt I owed them something.

When I deposited the big check in my checking account, I advised my banker that I would soon be transferring a substantial amount of it. I visited with my financial adviser and set up investment accounts for Red's two daughters, the four surviving grandchildren, and one great-grandchild. That child was born four months after his father, the fifth grandchild, died in a motorcycle crash. Red had felt so close to that little boy that I felt I had to treat him as a grandchild. Those accounts are also transferable on death.

When income tax time rolled around, I needed help, so I chose a certified public accountant to do my taxes. I could hardly understand some of the instructions. Red had often said that if he let me do the taxes, he'd have to visit me in jail. From then on, I compiled the worksheets and let Red do the major work.

I figured the CPA would be able to get me through a year or so. Not true. I trekked my way to his office every tax season.

I thought I had everything under control. Red had been gone for two and a half years, and the estate had been settled and the account closed for more than a year when I received a note from the Ohio Department of Taxation that I had overpaid his taxes in 2014 and I was due a refund.

The taxation people said the check was in the mail. The check was made out to Hugh M. Latimer dcd (deceased). Since the account was settled and the estate account closed, I sought advice from my bank. The woman advised me to return the check, explain about the estate account being closed, and ask if the check could be recut in my name. This is the same advice I got from the bank where Red had done his banking and where the estate account had been.

I hope this is the end of legal or financial entanglements.

Chapter 12

Vehicles

Another thing I had to deal with was all the motor vehicles we—now I—owned.

A 2002 Mercury Cougar—one of the last ones made—sat in the driveway, and a 2010 Lincoln MKX was parked in the garage beside my 2010 Ford Focus. Sitting in the parking area of a self-storage lot was a thirty-seven-foot motor home Red and I had purchased in the late 1980s. We hadn't used the motor home after the 2000 camping season because our last dog had died and camping wasn't the same without the dogs, Red said.

While it was at the storage space, the motor home had become a target of vandalism, even though Red had gone over regularly to start it and make sure things ran fine. A new door sat in the garage for what seemed like forever, and then one day it disappeared. Guess he managed to get it put on.

Come June 30, I stopped at the office of the self-storage lot to pay the rent. The people in the office said they were the new managers and they didn't know anything about the Latimer account or the motor home. It wasn't there.

How do you lose a thirty-seven-foot motor home? I asked myself. I had to put my investigative journalism talents to work.

I checked with the manufacturer. They didn't have any paperwork on it since it was so old and their computer didn't store information about vehicles that old.

I talked to the attorney's paralegal, and she advised me to locate the VIN (vehicle identification number) and said she'd try to trace it.

How do you lose a thirty-seven-foot motor home? kept going through my mind, even though I'd stumbled over United States Postal Service–type bins in the basement filled with items from the vehicle—kitchen utensils and odds and ends from drawers and storage areas. In the garage were canvas bags that held hoses, jumper cables, and things Red needed for mechanical purposes. A toolbox sat in his work area, making three such metal boxes I tripped over or struggled to move.

And I was still trying to find a thirty-seven-foot motor home. *Calm down,* I told myself. *Think.* I called the insurance company. Voilà! The agent still had the information on his computer and was able to share the VIN with me. I gave it to the paralegal. Not long after that, she discovered the motor home had a new owner.

But when? How? Did he donate it? Did he sell it? Why didn't he tell me? Did he think I knew what was happening when he brought things home? Did he have a senior moment and think he had told me even though he hadn't? I knew it wouldn't bring in much money because of its age and because it hadn't been used for so long, even though Red did start it and run it every month.

One thing satisfied me. It was gone and was one less thing I had to worry about.

Now moving on to the vehicles at home.

The Cougar didn't get driven much. By this time Red wasn't driving much anyway. Sort of like Grandma who only drove her car on Sundays.

He was also a bicycle rider. He started out hauling his bike on the back of the car. Later, when he bought a recumbent trike, he hauled it on a trailer. But that method took up too many spots in the parking lot. So off to the car dealer he went, looking for an SUV. That was about the only kind of vehicle he hadn't had. He bought a Ford Edge because it held his trike. We measured and measured to make sure it would fit.

But he wasn't fully satisfied with it, the main reason being that it wasn't red. It was beige. This would be the first vehicle he'd had in a long time that wasn't red. Then he began hanging out at the dealership looking for gently used red SUVs.

It wasn't long before he found the Lincoln MKX, the big SUV. We went for a ride the first night. I needed a step stool to get in (well, almost). He loved that SUV. He even made a wooden ramp to get the trike in and out of the back.

By the time he died, I had never driven the SUV. Nor had I even taken any vehicle in or out of that side of the garage. When he bought the house in late 1973, there was no garage. We had a two-car garage built on to the house, but we had to cut a few feet off to keep within property line limits. That meant the vehicle that went in that side of the garage went in and out at a slight angle.

My car went in straight on the side of the garage against the house. His went on the far side.

My car and the SUV resided in the garage; the Cougar stayed outside. I had a love–hate relationship with that car. I loved it because it was made in March 2002, near the end of the last run, and was almost a classic. I hated it because I sat very low in the seat, not far off the ground, and I had to pull the seat so far up to reach the pedals that the steering wheel was in my gut. Red didn't like me driving it much for fear that if I were in a crash, the airbag would hit me hard.

For those reasons the two vehicles weren't driven much after he died. And I didn't start them often enough, and the batteries went down. I had to have my road service folks out to jump the batteries.

I decided it was time to drive the SUV. I moved the Cougar and parked it on the street in front of the house. Then I backed my Focus out and parked it behind the Cougar. Now, after taking a deep breath, I carefully backed the Lincoln out of the garage. *Whew! That wasn't bad.*

I went for a short drive to get the feel of it. Soon I got brave enough to back it out with my car in the garage. I decided I'd sell the Cougar and keep the SUV.

Eventually I found a buyer for the Cougar. I did not want any nineteen-year-old who had already totaled one car to have this car. And I didn't want a sixteen-year-old newly licensed driver to have it either. I almost had it sold once, but the deal fell through. About a year after Red died, I finally found a buyer I could trust, one who really needed a car and could come up with the money. I sold it for a few dollars shy of the Kelley Blue Book price. The money went into the estate account.

The only thing remaining on the car agenda was to transfer the SUV over to me and then renew the license plates for both the SUV and my car. In Ohio we license our vehicles according to birth date. My and Red's birth dates were five weeks apart.

I could transfer the title at the auto title place and go next door to the Bureau of Motor Vehicles to renew the license plates.

No problem. Well, sort of no problem. The woman easily transferred the title over to me and gave me my copy. But she also began to ask questions about how and why Red died. I answered them vaguely as I always had. It was no concern of hers. I didn't feel comfortable with strangers wanting to know my personal history. I still don't feel comfortable talking about it. I guess it is the old stigma of suicide.

My next stop was next door at the Bureau of Motor Vehicles to renew the license plates for both the SUV and my Ford Focus. I couldn't believe I was now in full possession of two vehicles, one a Lincoln. I guess I had earned it.

I wanted to renew them both at once. Maybe I should have done them online as I did a year earlier. I'm sure it would have been emotionally easier, especially with the SUV. That was when the young woman behind the counter didn't understand the word *late* when she wanted Red's signature on the transfer papers.

Chapter 13

What Do You Do with a Personalized Leather Belt?

One of the hardest things I faced was what to do with Red's personal items and clothes.

This problem started upon his death and continued into … forever. Of course, some things I will keep and decide what to do with them as I get into my advanced years. But the other things?

Shortly after the body had been removed for its trip to the coroner's office, and once the sheriff's deputies finished with their work, I was all alone until my nephew arrived. I had gone into the back bedroom that Red had called his room. I studied the checkbook to see what I'd have to pay in the coming days.

As I turned to leave the room, that's when I found the combs. Those I soaked in hot soapy water and donated to the less fortunate.

He had so many clothes that I often suggested he donate what he wasn't wearing or going to wear again to a place that works with those less fortunate. He grumbled that he had once tried to give his sport coats to a shelter, but the people there hassled him so much that it wasn't worth it.

"I don't want to see bums wearing my clothes," he'd say.

"But you don't go in areas they do," I countered.

Now that Red was gone, I figured it was time to do something with the clothes. I started in the basement, where he had hung shirts he would wear around the house, or maybe wear them out, or hadn't had on since he moved them in back in the late fall of 1973.

I started by taking them off the hangers and washing them, long-sleeved ones first, then short-sleeved ones. I checked them for lost buttons, tears, ripped seams, and oil and grease stains. The damaged shirts got thrown out. Then I started folding and boxing up the remaining ones. One box. Two boxes. I counted fifty shirts. And a pile of hangers.

I took the fifty shirts over to my neighborhood thrift store. The young man who accepted them just opened the box, dumped the shirts in a pile, and gave me back the boxes. I wanted the boxes to fill for more donations.

I didn't like the way he'd treated the shirts, so I decided I'd take other donations elsewhere.

Another day I worked in the basement and opened the door of a cabinet in Red's workshop area. I found orange Gatorade lids. Why would anyone keep those unless there was a special project requiring them? Fortunately I was standing close to a trash can. Two handfuls of those orange lids went into that green trash can.

"A child of the Depression," my nephew Gavin said of Red when he visited a short time later.

How true. Red had been born in 1928, and much of his youth and growing-up period was during the Great Depression.

Bit by bit I went through drawers, closets, vehicles, and rooms, eventually thinking I had taken care of everything. I hadn't—and still haven't—gone into the room where he died. I just can't bring myself to go in there. It brings back too many memories.

One day I invited my friend and former coworker Rick out. I had some clothes I thought he could wear. I stopped him as he started up the steps into the living area. I opened the hall closet and began handing him clothes.

"If it fits, it's yours," I said.

When the leather jacket fit perfectly, he exclaimed, "I've never worn leather before."

"I'm not about to give a leather jacket to charity," I said.

This scene was repeated in the back room and in the basement.

When we got to the workshop area, Rick opened one cabinet door. There lay a Milky Way candy bar. *Geez, I'd finished Red's box of Milky War candy bars from the freezer months ago.*

Rick also meandered into the room where Red died. I asked him to count television sets. Every time a new TV came out on the market, Red would buy it. The one it replaced was relegated to the basement. Those, along with the TVs removed from the motor home, took up space in the basement. I counted eleven sets throughout the house, most of them analog. That number includes the ones I watch.

Little by little I was dispensing with items in the basement and in his back room.

I found lots of new clothes. Most of them I took to a Special Olympics drop box near the house. Special Olympics would sell them, and the money would be donated to the cause. A win-win situation. Someone got new clothes, probably not in the latest style, and Special Olympics got some money for its programs.

Other items from Red's main closet I took to the Methodist church where my support group meets. In my area the Methodist churches operate a free store for the less fortunate.

An unopened package of white tube socks became a Christmas gift. The hand-tooled leather belt with Red's name on still hangs in the closet, never having been worn.

All those tools in the basement! Stacks of cans that hold nails, screws, nuts, bolts. A lazy Susan with the same. A holder of drawers with different-size washers. At least three toolboxes so heavy I can hardly lift them. Perhaps a call to Habitat for Humanity.

I was able to sell a few items—the riding lawn mower and large snowblower. It's a start. Now to get busy dispensing with more items.

Every time I start complaining about not having these items out of the way, someone will say, "It takes time." Some of these people are speaking from experience.

Chapter 14

Sunday-Morning Breakfast

Red may be gone, but he's surely not forgotten. He's buried in a section of Green Lawn Cemetery that is easy to get to. I go there quite often and spend so much time each visit that I carry a lawn chair in both vehicles.

My first couple of visits I was still mad—so mad, in fact, that I stomped on the pile of dirt on his grave that had yet to settle. I was crying, "Get back here, and get me out of this mess!"

What mess I was in, I didn't know. All I knew was that I was alone, lonely, lonesome, and confused.

I handled the necessary actions with no problems—writing thank-you notes, paying bills, keeping track of checks I wrote and for what. I carried on with life the way it had been. I even kept up a few traditions the two of us had started.

Sunday mornings Red and I had breakfast together, the one day of the week neither of us had anything to do early in the day. I soon started going to the cemetery on Sunday mornings to have breakfast with him. He'd bought a big box of pastries at Sam's Club and left me with most of that box in the freezer. I'd take a pastry and stop at a convenience store near the cemetery for a cup of coffee. After juggling a cup of coffee and a pastry, I realized it would be easier to sit in a lawn chair, eat, and talk.

Regardless of what time I visit, I sit in the lawn chair, eat, drink, talk, and read out loud. It's quiet and peaceful. Sometimes I see a few deer. I usually go in the early morning, not long after the gates open, but at times I go for lunch.

I always bring him up to date on the goings-on, the deaths, sports actions, weather, news, or whatever I can think of. Sometimes I sound like a newscaster.

Often in February we have an unusually warm day. That's when Red and I would go on a picnic. We'd get the motor home out, buy subs, chips, and soft drinks, take the dogs with us, and spend the day in a state park. Now when that warm day in February rolls around, I buy a salad and soft drink and go to the cemetery for a picnic lunch.

I've had lunch on our anniversary and our birthdays, even the day he left me and the day I had him committed to the ground. I've taken a book I'm reading and read him a chapter. One Sunday morning as I was reading, a car stopped at my section and a woman got out. I stopped reading out loud as she approached me.

"I never thought of that," she said.

"What?" I responded. "The lawn chair or reading?"

"Both," she said, and turned around to go to her car.

When the Columbus Blue Jackets went on a great win streak in the 2016-17 season and soared to the top of the National Hockey League standings, I dug into my closet for the jersey Red had gotten me one year for Christmas. The jersey is a men's medium and way too big for me, so it was relegated to the back of the closet. But now I felt I needed to wear it. I got it out, rolled up the sleeves, and wore it. My first stop was at the cemetery to do a happy dance on his grave. "I'm wearing it! I'm wearing it!" I cried out.

I strive to keep the cemetery lot clean. Our markers are flush with the ground, which makes it easier for the grounds crew to mow. A vase chained to the holder between our markers holds artificial flowers and an American flag.

I've thought about purchasing a flag holder that depicts the war in which Red served. Only he didn't serve in a war. He was in the US Army and served in Korea, but not during a war. He enlisted after World War II was over and was discharged before the Korean War began. He did not see action.

He is considered a World War II veteran because he enlisted before December 31, 1946, the deadline the government set. He did get a draft notice for the Korean War, but his DD-214 meant he wouldn't be drafted.

I always said he was in a forgotten era—not World War II and not the Korean War. That's why I haven't been able to get a proper flag holder. The flag goes into the vase. I've tried to put a flag in the ground, but at times the ground was too dry and hard.

The first Veterans Day after Red's death, the flag I put in the vase was plastic. I cried because people would think I was cheap.

Some people I know who have a loved one buried not too far away tell me they wave and say hi to Red as they drive past my section. Most of the people I see at the cemetery are women.

I've also had people tell me they are afraid of cemeteries. Not I. I lived next door to a cemetery when I was growing up, and as a young teenager, I mowed the grounds. And I've come to appreciate the history behind—or underneath—the markers.

Chapter 15

What Do I Do Now on Holidays?

Holidays are the hardest is something I heard from people who have been through the loss of a spouse.

My first test was the Fourth of July. My nephew Gavin threw a birthday party for his daughter Stephanie, who would be two that year. The previous year Red and I went out midafternoon for the party, the cake and ice cream, and the opening of gifts.

In 2014 I went for much of the day. Gavin lives on the parade route in his community. I ate breakfast casserole and a goopy doughnut while sitting on a lawn chair on the curb watching the parade. A cup of coffee sat at my feet. What a different way to have breakfast or watch a parade!

In my community on the other end of town, our Independence Day parade is the last Saturday morning in June. It ends at the fire department, where there is a fish fry.

After watching the parade at Gavin's, I stirred the food for lunch and helped my nephew's mother-in-law clean the kitchen as I got to know her better. I also got to meet some of my nephew's family on his mother's side and his friends. By midafternoon, my niece Shannon and her husband, Zac, arrived with the cake, and the birthday party for Stephanie began. I didn't stay to watch the community fireworks.

For Red's birthday that August I bought a salad and a drink at a sandwich shop near the cemetery and sat at the grave and had my picnic. For my birthday, the day was just another day.

But Veterans Day got to me. I wanted to make sure Red had a flag on his grave. The marker was in place, and I could put a flag in the ground. I had a couple of flags in that overstuffed Fibber McGee's Closet,[1] but when I pulled them out I discovered they were plastic, not cloth. I put one in the ground anyway. Then I started to cry. Was it because Red liked Veterans Day, or was it because of the plastic flag?

Red looked forward to Veterans Day because restaurants had begun offering free sandwiches or meals for veterans. He'd always selected his restaurant and had his DD-214 (honorable discharge papers) ready.

"Don't fix me anything for supper," he'd say. "I'm going out."

I never asked to join him; Veterans Day was his day.

Now this Veterans Day I cried. I cried the next couple of days.

The second Veterans Day alone really hit me. I cried. No, I sobbed. I almost choked on my sobs. This went on for three days. *Get it out!* I told myself. *Let it all out!* I leaned against the wall in the hallway and sobbed. I gave up on using tissues and went for the paper towels to wipe my tears and blow my nose.

For Thanksgiving, I still go to Mount Victory, where Red grew up. I meet his niece and nephew and their families for dinner at the Plaza, the popular busy restaurant down the road from where Red lived as a child. I stop at the graves of his parents although they had passed on long before I married into the family. I also visit a second cemetery, where the graves of a couple of Red's classmates are. He had a set of twins in his class, and they told us where they would be buried. We knew one of the twins in his class had died but hadn't heard from or about the other one. The second year I visited that cemetery alone, I discovered the second twin had died—the day after Red. How weird I felt standing there and seeing the date.

Thanksgiving dinner with Red's family at that restaurant is a buffet. There is good food and plenty of it. I was able to get my fill of pea salad and sliced bananas in caramel sauce. We all make sure we get to the sliced bananas.

---

[1] *Fibber McGee and Molly* was a popular radio show running from 1935 to 1956. The overstuffed hall closet was a running gag in the show. When the closet was mentioned, listeners could hear the many items fall out. Hence, any overstuffed closet, which many people have, is nicknamed Fibber McGee's Closet.

For Christmas I was invited to Gavin's aunt's house. But first I gave my service to the Meals on Wheels program at LifeCare Alliance. I assisted another woman in getting the drivers started on their routes.

As Red and I had done for several years, I went to Sandusky the day after Christmas to see his daughters and their families.

Valentine's Day brought lots of memories. One year Valentine's Day fell close to the Mardi Gras celebration. I had been in Pensacola, Florida, and Orange Beach, Alabama, the year before and enjoyed king cake. Down there, people celebrate Mardi Gras from Epiphany to Ash Wednesday. The following year I was able to get a king cake in Columbus. This one resembled the cinnamon bread we'd bought from the traveling bakery truck when I was a kid. Red and I enjoyed it so much that for Valentine's Day, he went to the grocery store and bought a second one. This one was my Valentine's Day present, he said. The following day he went to the store and bought the last one. It was almost stale, but he said it would be good to dunk in hot coffee or tea.

Another year when he came to breakfast, I was in the kitchen reading the paper at the counter, waiting for him to get up. He walked into the kitchen and slid two frozen Milky Way candy bars across the counter. "Don't say I didn't give you chocolate for Valentine's Day."

I looked at him, giggled, and said, "You funny bunny." I always said that to him when he did something funny.

At holidays, my nephew's aunt Liz made sure I wasn't forgotten. She invited me for Christmas and for Easter. We all participated in Easter egg hunts. Gifts inside the eggs vary according to age. We big "children" might find a small bottle of spirits inside an egg instead of bubble gum or a toy.

By the time Memorial Day rolled around, I had purchased a few cloth flags at the fabric and craft store in the nearby shopping center. Red had a cloth flag for Memorial Day. These days I have a couple of cloth flags in both vehicles.

For my birthday in the fall of 2015, I felt much better and more secure. I realized I didn't have anyone to take me to dinner or buy me a cake, which Red often did. I decided I'd throw my own birthday party.

I picked the restaurant and bought a cake. The first person I invited didn't like the restaurant I chose, so she didn't want to go to lunch. I called another person, and she jumped at the chance. The next year I invited some friends and my nephew and his family to a hot-dog-based restaurant. What fun we had!

Now that I'm alone, I've learned to do things a little differently at times. I'll still do some of the traditional things, but I'm willing to start new ones.

Not long after I calmed down after the funeral, I asked a friend who had lost her husband many years before how and why she signed up as a volunteer for the Meals on Wheels program. She chose to volunteer on holidays because she didn't have much of a family. *I can do that,* I thought. That's why I volunteer at Meals on Wheels on holidays.

On Valentine's Day I've counted out carnations for each route where they are donated for the clients. I've counted valentines made by schoolchildren, and at Easter I've counted little baskets Girl Scouts have fixed for the clients.

At least I don't feel as though I'm alone on holidays. LifeCare Alliance is around the corner from the cemetery. I'll have my breakfast with Red and then go help out at Meals on Wheels.

Chapter 16

I Have to Take Care of Myself

I'd been doing so much for Red and attending to other aspects of life that I nearly forgot about myself.

I had the estate to work on. I kept up with my work assignments. And I kept trying to lead my own life as though nothing had happened, but deep down I was living with the horrors of what did happen. I had a lot of decisions to make, not only decisions that I normally would have made but now also decisions that Red would have made. I was thinking for two people but acting as one. And I was trying to take over the work Red used to do around the house.

Fortunately Dion, who had so graciously handled the funeral service, volunteered to mow my yard for the summer. One less thing I had to worry about, because a sore shoulder meant I couldn't pull-start the mower. That lasted into the summer of 2015, when Dion advised me he and his family were moving out of the neighborhood that fall. I'd either have to learn to start the mower or get someone to mow my yard. Another expense.

I already faced property taxes, auto insurance, homeowners' insurance, and utility bills. The electric bill went down somewhat because the TV wasn't going all day long. And the water usage would go down too.

Then there was all the housework. Running the sweeper. Dusting. Cleaning up the kitchen after I prepared a meal. I realized how much Red once did around the house. After he retired he took on the duties of running the sweeper on a regular basis and doing some other household

66

chores. He even liked short trips to the grocery store. He did his laundry. He did the outdoor work. It seemed as though he was always tinkering with something. Even if a light bulb burned out, he would have it changed before I could get to the supply of light bulbs to change it myself.

Before the end of the first month after burying Red, I had my regular quarterly doctor's appointment. Jenny, the nurse whom Red and I had known long enough that she didn't mind my calling her Vampire Jenny, drew blood each visit. I'd remembered to drink plenty of liquids the day before to hydrate myself and make it easier for her to draw the necessary three vials of blood.

The three vials were needed for a CBC—a complete blood count—which would help determine if anything in my system was out of whack. The test would be done and the results mailed to me. After all I'd been through over the years, I knew where my numbers should be.

I'd had intravenous chemotherapy after being diagnosed with ovarian cancer in the fall of 1982. I later learned I have serpentine veins. My veins snake their way down my arm instead of going straight, so this gives nurses a headache when trying to get a needle in a vein.

These quarterly doctor appointments with a blood draw began in 2004 when I had suffered a myocardial infarction and undergone an emergency quadruple bypass. Doctors then advised me to avoid red meat and caffeine. Chicken and fish replaced beef. I learned to drink decaffeinated coffee. I started fixing two types of meals—one for Red and one for me. I worked my way back into walking long distances—walking past one more house each day in my neighborhood. I needed to do that daily walking again.

Shortly after Red's passing, the doctor noticed a slight rise in my glucose level. An A1C was added. This is a test to check the glucose or sugar level in the blood over a period of time—for me, every three months.

"Eat more vegetables" was the advice from the doctor. Diet and exercise. Add another layer of vegetables to that tossed salad I was eating for lunch. Head lettuce, chopped cabbage, chopped broccoli salad, julienne carrots, cut-up cauliflower florets, cucumbers, often a hard-boiled egg, raisins or Craisins. Oh yes, watch the amount of dressing.

I even steamed or cooked some frozen vegetables to go with some pieces of chicken I'd microwave for dinner or with baked fish pieces. I cut back on potatoes and pasta. I rarely made my delicious macaroni and cheese or baked a potato in the microwave.

I made a concentrated effort to eat at regular hours, but with my schedule, I had difficulties. Still the glucose level was rising.

"Let's see if we can get it under control with medication," the doctor said as the word *diabetes* crept into our discussions. Another prescription went to my corner pharmacy.

Three months later, my glucose level and A1C were still higher than what we wanted. The visit nearest the anniversary of Red's death brought about emotional feelings.

"Thoughts of suicide?" my doctor asked.

"Oh, no," I quickly replied, knowing I hadn't said anything to her or anyone else as to the cause of Red's death.

Diet—did I say I like some sweets now and then? Exercise—I had stopped taking my long walks and had to get back into it. Medication— add another pill to the number I was taking. Finally, after putting it off as long as I could, I accepted the order to start finger-stick blood tests twice a day to monitor my glucose level. I had a history of dreading needles. Not long after that I was referred to an endocrinologist.

Now I really had to admit I was a type 2 diabetic. *How did this happen? How and when did my body stop making insulin or reduce the amount it was making?* I was trying hard to keep my numbers where they should be. Really, I was!

The first visit to the endocrinologist resulted in another prescription, and the second visit produced the order to do nightly injections of insulin with the Lantus pen. The pharmacist had taught me to do the daily finger sticks when I picked up the glucometer. The endocrinologist's nurse taught me to do the injections in my abdominal area.

Eventually my glucose level and A1C level started falling.

Needless to say, I'd had a lot of stress in my life, and that's not always easy to control.

In the fall of 2015 I had to clean the yard one afternoon so the lawn care company could put a fall treatment on the lawn the next day. I raked and bagged four bags of leaves. By the time I got inside, my shoulders ached so bad I was near tears. I started searching for a massage.

When I worked at Ohio State in the 1990s, a secretary in our department had a regular massage. *That's what I need,* I told myself. I put it off. I often thought about getting a gift certificate for a massage for Red for a gift-giving occasion, but I knew what he'd say—*Here, you use it*—and then hand it back to me.

I'd had a massage a year earlier when I visited my friend Rosemary in Albany, New York. I felt relieved afterward, albeit a little sore because the therapist worked areas not touched in the past.

I got my massage and signed up for one the next month. As I lay on the table and let the massage therapist work on me, I thought of how many times I had considered getting Red a gift certificate for a massage. *Had I gone through with getting that certificate, might I not have lost him the way I did? When his legs started hurting, could I have gotten him in for a massage? Would it have helped his back or his legs? But then again, as stubborn as he was those last days, he probably wouldn't have gone.*

I now go every month for a massage. It's an hour I know I can relax.

After overcoming a disastrous 2014, I looked forward to a better 2015. But I developed cataracts on both eyes and had to have them removed. I had to find someone who was free those days and who could take me for those surgeries.

Maybe 2016 would be better. But then my mammogram showed something unusual, and I underwent a lumpectomy. Two surgeries more. Again I had to find someone who was available to take me for outpatient surgery and drive me home. Fortunately the abnormality was diagnosed as in situ. The bad cells had not escaped the duct. *Dodged that bullet.*

One afternoon in late summer 2016 I was walking with a nurse friend, and she asked the quintessential question—"How are you getting along?" As we talked about my stress after Red's death and the resulting diabetes, she said, "That's understandable."

Maybe 2017. While on my usual midwinter break to Florida, I overdid the walking and started having breathing problems. I felt like I did in 2013 when I had congestive heart failure and fluid on the lungs. I decided to stop at the hospital en route home to get checked out for what I thought was congestive heart failure. I got home three days later. All they found was a rapid heartbeat.

In 2018, I thought I had it made. No hospital trip. But December 1, I was pulled over after becoming lost and confused. The two law enforcement officers persuaded me to go to the hospital. A CT scan ruled out a stroke and an EEG ruled out seizures. However, my ammonia count was high. Three days later I got to go home and left doctors trying to figure out the cause of the elevated ammonia.

Maybe 2019.....

Chapter 17

Can We Find Another Word for *Widow?*

In the fall of 2014 I was standing at the front storm door looking for squirrels. I was a couple of steps away from where I had sat when I spoke to the 911 operator that fateful day. I often stand at the front door to watch squirrels and birds and to watch the clouds roll by.

I got to thinking as I stood there. *I'm a widow. What a horrible word.*

Visions of those colonial women in their black dresses entered my mind. Even Scarlett O'Hara Hamilton in her black dress tapping her toes to the music at the bazaar. Back in those days mourning women wore black for at least a year. I do have a black dress, but I rarely wear a dress these days.

Back in 2008 Red's grandson Chris was killed in a motorcycle accident. As we were getting ready to go to the memorial service, Red asked, "Do you have a dress?" I had worn slacks for so long that he wondered what all was in my closet. That day I wore that black dress, and I haven't had it on since.

I didn't wear that black dress to Red's funeral. I wore a blue dress, one that has seen a lot of funeral duty. I wore it to a friend's service and also to my mother's funeral.

I'm too young to be a widow. Are there any age guidelines to widowhood? I'm in my early seventies, but in my mind, and judging by the music that runs through my mind, I'm still back in my teen years and hearing music of the early days of rock and roll.

I hate the word *widow.* I wish we could remove it from the English language.

The first time I had to fill out a form and had to check a marital box, I was shaking as I put my *X* in the box marked "widow."

I go somewhere and I'm referred to as Mrs. Latimer. *Who am I?* Society needs a new word. When a woman is unmarried, growing up, she is Miss So-and-So. When she marries, she becomes a missus. But what do you call a woman who has lost her husband, or even one who has divorced?

I'm not a "miss," and I'm no longer a missus. *What am I?* Ms., à la Gloria Steinem? I don't like that appellation either.

I like a friend's idea. She maintains she is Walter's wife. "I was never his widow; I was his wife," she still says many years after his death.

And that brings up another question: What do you do with the rings?

I still wear my rings, mainly because I can't get them off. The wedding band is a plain circle, but the engagement ring is a one-carat heart-shaped diamond. I had heard about this cut in 1972 and thought it sounded neat. If ever I had the opportunity, that was what I would choose. And it's what I got.

If I were to have these rings removed, probably cut off, what would I do with my diamond? Put it in the safe-deposit box? Why not wear it as long as I can? I know whom it's going to when I leave earth.

Red's ring, that's another story. At the conclusion of the service, the funeral director removed Red's wedding ring and Ohio Highway Patrol ring, put them in a blue velvet string purse, and handed them to me before we left for the cemetery. I put the wedding ring on the chain I was wearing. I wore it every day. One day the chain opened and fell off. I couldn't find the ring for ten days. I started wearing it again once I found it. Fourteen months after Red's passing, I got out of the car in a park in Fairborn and discovered the chain open and hanging around my neck. No ring. I searched the car. Still no ring.

It's gone. Just like his first one, the one I gave him at the wedding. One cold winter morning we were out running errands. I found his patrol ring on the car floor, like it had slipped off his cold finger when he removed his glove. He looked all over and couldn't find his wedding ring. A few days later we went to a local jeweler, and Red selected a new ring. "I like this one better than I liked the first one," he said.

I felt bad about losing his ring—like I had let him down, like I was clumsy, not caring.

What surviving spouses do with their rings is their choice. I asked a former coworker a few years after his wife passed what he did with the rings. "I tossed them in a drawer," he said. Talking about this situation one day among a group of women, one older woman waved her hand in front of me, and I saw rings that showed age. "I'm still wearing mine," she said. I then felt it was okay to wear mine. I'll wear mine as long as is proper.

Should I remarry, of course, I would remove them. I have reservations there. I'm receiving widows' benefits (I prefer survivors' benefits, but that includes children, which Red and I didn't have) from both the highway patrol and the bank. I would lose them if I were to remarry. What would I get in return?

Chapter 18

I'm Sorry I Put You through That

Once I agreed to the autopsy, I sort of forgot about it. The autopsy was performed, and the body was released to the funeral home in time for embalming and the Friday service.

A part of the autopsy was a toxicology test, which takes a good six weeks for the results to come in. After six weeks I called the coroner's office. I was told it would be a while yet.

"You must be busy," I said, getting a "Yes, we are" answer.

A couple of weeks later a thick envelope from the coroner's office came in the mail. It was the autopsy report. Part of me wanted to rip it open and read it right away. Another part of me thought, *No. Calm down. Then open it gently and read it.*

The second paragraph of the cover page identified Red as married, eighty-five years of age, a resident of Columbus, Ohio, of the white race, with blue eyes and gray hair, clean-shaven, measuring 71 inches in length, and weighing 111 pounds.

One hundred and eleven pounds! That's less than what I weigh! His weight in the forty years I knew him had been around 180 pounds or so. *How did he lose that much weight? Why didn't I see it? Was I too wrapped up in my life to notice what was happening to him?* He was eating, but reduced portions by choice. He once showed me where he had put a new hole in his belt. That weight helps explain the comment one of our friends made the day of the funeral: "He looks so thin."

But 111 pounds! Was he weighed *after* the organs were removed during the autopsy? His organs were weighed in grams, but the conversion from pounds to kilograms and vice versa didn't compute for overall weight.

At the bottom of the page, it listed cause of death. That I already knew. I had to go deeper into the remaining four pages, front and back.

I moved on to the second page, a chart of basic information.

Getting into the remaining pages meant I needed a dictionary. *Where is our* Webster's Dictionary? *It had sat on the dining room table within easy reach when we needed it for crossword puzzles or other reference work when reading the paper, but where did I put it in the rush to clean up after he died?* I searched two places before I found it, not under the desktop computer table but in the Fibber McGee's overstuffed closet.

Although I had worked in medical communications for eight years and I knew some of the terms, I really needed help with reading the autopsy report. *Do I need a standard dictionary, or do I need the medical dictionary/ encyclopedia?*

I looked up such words as *cardiomegaly* (enlarged heart) and *calvarium* (upper domed part of the skull).

The external examination showed nothing out of the ordinary. Scars from Red's hernia surgeries were noted. In the section marked "Evidence of Injury," the gunshot wound report was extensive with descriptions of the entrance wound, the path of the bullet, and the exit wound, and mentioned hemorrhaging around the two holes.

Did he suffer? How long did he live after he pulled the trigger? Was death instantaneous? Did it hurt?

For the internal examination, the usual Y-shaped incision was made. That's the cut made into the chest so the internal organs can be examined. The words *normal* and *glistening* showed up in each paragraph. But when it came to the head, I began to shake. The top of the head had to be removed to take out the brain. The report mentioned "converging circular saws."

Oh. My. God! Did they use saws on you like you have in your basement workshop? What did I do to you? The report sounded so gruesome that it upset me. I cried, thinking of all he went through. And to think I had made the decision to put him through all that. But I needed to know if there was an underlying cause. The autopsy didn't show anything that I was looking for.

If I had it to do over, I would not opt for the autopsy. I am so sorry for what I did to him.

When the funeral home called to tell me the body had arrived, embalmed and ready for Friday's service, I asked one big question: "Is he suitable for showing?" I was advised he was. When I viewed the body at the funeral home, I saw no evidence of a gunshot wound or of the cut to remove the brain (which at that time I didn't know about).

Either the physician who performed the autopsy did a terrific job of putting him back together or the funeral home had done a good job. Maybe both. Was he sewn up, or was he glued together? Visitors couldn't see anything either. At least they didn't say anything to me.

Shortly after the autopsy report arrived, I made arrangements to go to Sandusky to visit with my stepdaughters. Marsha and I sat at Marlene's dining table and went over the report. Marsha is a retired nurse and knew a lot of medical things, much more than I did. Nothing stood out to her in her perusal.

"I can't believe he had the courage to pull the trigger," she commented.

Chapter 19

Many Do Complete Suicide

Suicide is more prevalent than many people think. We don't hear much about it unless the person is well-known or the situation is unusual or occurs in a news-making way.

The death of comedy actor Robin Williams made the news because he was a celebrity. A suicide by someone holed up in a house while a SWAT team tries to get him or her out and the person inside kills himself or herself makes the news. A returning serviceman taking his life because he can't adjust to life at home after having seen atrocities abroad has become news.

But how many John or Jane Q. Publics in the list of death notices in the daily newspaper are people who completed suicide? We'll probably never know, because the cause of death is rarely mentioned by the media or in the death notices.

In 2014, the year Red shot himself, 169 other people died by their own hand, according to the Franklin County Coroner's Office. That's about one every couple of days.

Franklin County is in central Ohio, and Columbus, the state capital, is the county seat. According to figures released in 2018, the Metropolitan Columbus area, which stretches into neighboring counties, sports just over two million people.

Also in 2014, the age of suicide victims in the county ranged from preteen to over seventy, and in Red's case, he was well over seventy. Seventy-three of the people died by firearms, forty-nine hanged themselves, thirty-three died by other means, and fifteen deaths listed as suicide had undetermined causes. As for other means, the coroner's office considers the deaths to be by intoxication, asphyxia (too little oxygen and too much carbon dioxide in the blood), drowning, exsanguination (loss of blood), stabbing, and strangulation. Caucasian males made up the largest number of suicides.

Franklin County had recorded 174 suicides in 2012, but that number dropped to 156 in 2013. It rose in 2014 and again in 2015 to 178. It's ironic that suicides outnumber homicides.

Figures from the coroner's office show that in 2015, the county recorded 125 homicides and 178 suicides. The local media counts the homicides and the public becomes outraged, but no one counts the suicides other than the coroner's office.

The rise in suicides is not only local. Figures from the National Center for Health Statistics show that nationally suicide is on the rise. The rate in 2014 was 24 percent higher than it was in 1999, and the greatest rise was in young teens, for which segment of the population the rate doubled in that fifteen-year span. These figures also show that most men who took their own lives did so by firearms, while poison was the choice of women. A similar report in 2018 shows suicides on the rise in Ohio.

Even though people say there is a problem with the large number of military personnel taking their own lives, a report from the Centers for Disease Control and Prevention in January 2016 said that military rates were similar to civilian rates.

This report noted an increase in active-duty personnel but a decrease in the national guard and reserves. The army had the highest rates, and the navy had the lowest.

January is a big month for suicide. I can understand that. The holidays are over. Relatives have returned home. Gone is the glitter of the season. Outside is an overcast sky, at least in central Ohio. Does the pain someone is facing cause him or her to suffer depression? *Was Red in a depression? I believe so, although it didn't show up on the autopsy. How could it show up?*

No one wants to believe that anyone in their family will be among those statistics. I have to admit that the possibility Red would commit suicide did cross my mind. I had thought that someday I would come home to find him dead of suicide. I thought he would hang himself. I never thought he would do it by gunfire. He had too much respect for guns. Yet he knew a lot about firearms.

He had carried a weapon during his nearly twenty-five years with the Ohio Highway Patrol and had access to weapons during his sixteen years at the bank. He was required to go through a shooting regimen once a year with these jobs, and he shot occasionally at the range where he volunteered. After shooting, he'd sit in the middle of the living room floor with his cleaning equipment and talk about his day. For years his bullet-riddled targets from the patrol shoot hung on the basement wall.

Not long after he retired from the bank, he began volunteering at the shooting range where law enforcement officers qualified for their federal concealed-carry weapons cards.

I tried to search for answers as to why he shot himself. All I could think of was that he wanted to escape the pain he was experiencing. But I wanted to go deeper. Did the pain send him into depression?

I had other questions too. Did he die instantly? Did he suffer? Did he realize what he had done and want to reverse his decision?

But I asked myself a lot of questions too. *How did I miss the signs of pain that may have sent him into depression? Could I have prevented this? Even if I had found someone who could have offered help, could I have gotten him to go? I doubt that.*

Forty-six years earlier did Red try to get help for his second wife before she took her life in much the same way he later did? It must have hurt him tremendously, because he didn't speak about it much. Joyce had cystic fibrosis, a breathing condition. He said she was in pain and couldn't take it any longer. It was awhile after we were married that he told me about her shooting herself. Then he experienced a rapid heartbeat, and I thought I'd have to take him to the hospital. I never asked prying questions because I didn't want to hurt him or send him into another episode of a rapid heartbeat.

Many years into our marriage we learned his brother Wayne in California had died of a combination of liquor and pills. Red had considered that a suicide.

Chapter 20

We Suffer from PTSD

Much has been written and said of late about PTSD—post-traumatic stress disorder. It's generally been associated with a military environment. It's nothing new. It's been around for a long time, under different names.

In World War I and World War II, the service personnel experienced many atrocities of battle—the shooting, the bombing, watching their buddies die gruesome deaths. What they suffered was called "shell shock" at that time. Many servicemen relived the action and had so many other reactions.

Only in later years, after Vietnam and with the fighting in the Middle East and Afghanistan did we come to know it as PTSD.

Servicemen and servicewomen are given some time off—rest and relaxation, known as R&R, a time to get away from battle. But for some, the memories of what they went through will always haunt them.

Going through traumatic experiences is not limited to military personnel. Both men and women in everyday life experience traumatic events. Many women, I learned at a conference where I heard a psychiatrist speak, consider such events a part of life. Is that why more men than women report having experienced PTSD and seek treatment or counseling?

Looking back on my own life, I wonder how many traumatic experiences I have gone through. The loss of my father when I was sixteen. Major surgery when I was thirty-nine where ovarian cancer was found. A myocardial infarction that resulted in a quadruple bypass when I was sixty. And now the loss of my husband after forty years of marriage.

I've had my share—or more, I guess—of traumatic experiences. I've handled them well and moved on with my life.

The death of a loved one is definitely a traumatic event. It's hard for anyone to lose a loved one, whether it is a spouse, a child, or a parent. My heart goes out to all of them. We all know that we're going to lose a loved one, and we don't really know when. The survivors grieve in their own way.

My heart also goes out to those who lose a loved one in a natural way. My mother, for instance, lost two husbands. Both times she was sitting bedside as these wonderful men drew their last breaths. She had sort of been prepared. Me, on the other hand, I lost a wonderful man by surprise and so suddenly and so tragically that I was in no way prepared. My being thrown into widowhood was like being picked up by a tornadic wind and deposited in another field. I think losing a loved one by his or her own hand or in an accident is harder on the survivors than is losing someone who dies a natural death.

I do relive that day quite often. I still cry occasionally. I visit the cemetery a few times a month. I'm not alone in reliving the fateful day. Others in my situation, I have learned, relive the day they lost their loved one.

Some survivors seek counseling. Others do not. I'm not here to judge or tell anyone what they should do. I just carried on with my life. I felt that was what I should do. Anything else would have been out of character for me.

But I did find a support group, Survivors of Suicide Bereavement Support Group. One thing we have talked about is writing, or journaling, as a way to work through our grief.

Chapter 21

Survivors of Suicide Offer Help

A few days after the burial, I received a letter from the coroner's office. It was too quick for the autopsy report to be finished, and the envelope was too thin.

It was a list of support groups. *Just what I need,* I thought sarcastically. Then I remembered a sympathy card from a friend who had lost her husband in a tragic way contained a handwritten note suggesting that I find a support group.

My eyes scanned down this list. It contained both general support groups and death-specific groups. I recognized the location of some of the numbers, but with the proliferation of cell phones, it was difficult to tell which neighborhood some of the numbers were from. I put the letter aside.

A few days later I got a package from a local and well-respected mental health office. Inside this manila envelope was a list of Survivors of Suicide (SOS) bereavement support groups. One group met every Thursday night, a night I just happened to be free, and at a church near me. On Thursday nights no meetings were scheduled that I'd have to cover for the weekly newspaper for which I had been writing the past dozen or so years.

I decided to go to this support group meeting, but I was determined to sit back and listen to these people and not talk. I wanted to learn. But that plan didn't last long.

I walked into the room where a half dozen or so people sat around a table, with doughnuts in the center. Soft drinks were in a cooler at the foot of the table. I put a powdered doughnut on a napkin in front of me and got a soft drink.

Around the table they went, introducing themselves and telling about losing a loved one to suicide. Joy, the woman who started this group, was sitting beside me. These people had each lost a child or another relative. I was the only one who'd lost a spouse. Much to my surprise, I spoke openly about what had happened. I spoke in a strong voice. I didn't stammer, and my voice didn't crack. It surprised even me.

I felt that having someone take his or her own life was akin to the scarlet letter *A* that Hester Prynne wore on her dress. I had told family members but kept quiet with the neighbors and among friends because I didn't want incorrect information being circulated. Nor did I want to be singled out or have fingers pointed at me.

And here I was among strangers talking so freely about how Red suffered, how I reacted when I found him, and how nicely I was treated by first responders. I hoped that what was said there stayed there.

The week after that meeting, I wrestled with going back.

No, I'm not going back. All they talked about was the past. I need to move on, I thought.

They were talking about the past to let you know how they got to where they are today, I added.

Back and forth I went on this issue. The next Thursday I went back. Garry, Joy's husband, greeted me with a hug. *I needed that.* I joined the conversation. Week after week I showed up. I shared with refreshments, many times taking freshly made baked goods—coffee cake, pumpkin cupcakes, occasionally a pie. I learned that the first week of the month is set aside for pizza and soft drinks. Garry makes a pot of coffee.

One week they asked me if I wanted to join them the following Tuesday on an overnight fishing trip to Lake Erie. I don't fish, but I could have called the kids in Sandusky. *If these people had given me more notice, I could have rescheduled my newspaper assignments.*

"Next time, give me a little more notice," I said.

In late September I took in a little cake that I had bought at my neighborhood supermarket and had the bakery department write "Happy Birthday" on it. Garry's brother Larry brought in a birthday cake. Mine was white; his was chocolate. Come to find out, we share a birthday, but I'm one year older.

Over time we've welcomed several survivors of suicide. We share experiences, including how we're coping and what gets us through. We celebrate little victories with hugs. And we offer hugs and encouragement for setbacks.

These people have become like family. I look forward to spending ninety minutes with them every week. If I can't make the meeting, I always let the leader know. We're all friends on Facebook with each other.

One night when I walked into the room, I was greeted with "I know you" from a first-time couple. Pat explained they were in a group that I had given a tour to when I worked at Green Lawn Cemetery.

"We've learned to laugh," one woman told a newcomer one night.

We've discussed why our loved ones did what they did. The *why* is so hard to understand. I know Red was in pain. And when I think of this, that's when I remember that he said if he ever found himself in pain, "I'd off myself."

I also wondered why he used a gun since he had so much respect for firearms. One woman suggested it might be because he had so much experience with firearms. He had learned to use field guns as a young man hunting; he had been exposed to firearms with the patrol and with the bank in a security position; he engaged in regular shooting practice; and he volunteered at a shooting range.

One man talked about his son shooting himself and spoke about the smell of gunpowder. There was that smell I couldn't immediately define as I went down the steps that fateful day. *How could I not have recognized that smell after all the trapshooting I had done with my stepfather when I was in my early twenties? I guess my olfactory organ didn't retain that smell.*

We also talk about our feelings, problems we've encountered, or something we heard or saw during the week that sent us into a tailspin, sent us into a bout of depression, or made us feel good. Everybody has something to say.

Occasionally we'll talk about those who may have attempted suicide before and were taken to a hospital.

Often someone will say that a medical professional should attend our session. I finally did mention it to my doctor, but she hasn't shown up. Once a nursing student visited our group to listen to what we had to say.

At the end of the meeting, everyone gets and gives a hug.

I look forward to Thursday nights and often tell people I can't do something with them on that night because it is when my support group meets. It's my new family. It's the glue that's holding me together.

At times when we haven't been able to meet at the church, we've met at a restaurant for dinner or in someone's backyard for a picnic. We've even gone on a week's vacation together.

Sometimes I feel that not enough attention is paid to suicide. I realize we survivors relive the day our loved ones chose to leave us, but we need to move forward. The rate of suicide, about one every couple of days, I feel is too high and should be made known. As time goes on, I find myself wanting to talk more openly about what happened that day and the weeks leading up to it.

We survivors are all different, but we all share one thing. It's something we know we'll never get over, but at least we're getting through it.

Chapter 22

Reflections: What If and What Is

We writers play the what-if game every time we sit down to do creative writing. The rules are simple: Here is the situation. Now, what if this happens. How does the situation change?

I've played that game in real life many times since June 9, 2014, and I probably will continue to play it.

What if I had been able to get Red to go to his doctor? Would he have let me go with him? Would he have gone by himself?

What if I had caught him with the gun? Would I have had the nerve and strength to wrest it away from him and persuade him not to use it? Would things have escalated and the outcome have been different?

What if I had wakened him that last morning? I could have lived with his grumbling of "You know I don't feel good. I don't want to be bothered when I don't feel good." Instead I have to live with his decision to end it all a short time later.

What if I hadn't gone to HandsOn that morning? I went because I felt I needed a respite. Was I thinking too much of myself?

What if he had confided in me that he had suicidal thoughts and intentions? Could I have found him help? And in time?

What was on his mind in those last hours? Was it me? Was it just his agonizing pain? How long did he lie there before he pulled the trigger? Did he struggle with his decision?

What if he hadn't taken the path he did? How long would he have lived? Would those leg shocks really have worn his body down—just like I had told a lot of people?

Every time I get a massage, I think about Red's aches and pains. Would a massage have helped him?

I've beaten myself up so many times that I can't count that high. But there's nothing I can do about it. What's past is past.

Just about every day I thank myself for that last kiss. As I walked past him in his recliner Sunday evening, I stopped, put my arms around his neck, leaned over, and kissed his forehead.

Now I have to get on with my life. I've tried to do that as best as I can.

One of the first things I did was talk with my neighbors about their security alarms. I decided I had to have one installed.

That was my first big decision. Friends had told me I needed to get an alarm system. I was able to assure them that I had thought of that before I buried Red. The system was installed before the end of summer.

Do I sleep better knowing my doors and windows are alarmed when it gets dark? I don't think so, because too many other variables factor into getting a good night's sleep.

I'm making progress. I sold the car, learned to drive the SUV, and took time to trim the yard after someone mowed it. Gone are the many to-do lists; however, one surfaces when I'm getting ready to go somewhere or do something special and I know so much has to be done. Or when I'm thinking about what I have to pack.

I also have my weak moments.

High school football season starts in mid-August. I go to games in my district. I have the Top 55 card that gives me free admission to school activities. *One perk of getting older.* Or I go to games in another conference, one that accepts the Golden Buckeye Card as admission for us older people. *Another perk.*

I remember the day my Golden Buckeye Card arrived. We Ohioans get that card when we turn sixty, and it's good for discounts at many places, even granting free admission to athletic events in certain conferences.

Red got the mail that day. He recognized the return address on the envelope. He stood on the front stoop, opened the storm door, and yelled,

"Your Golden Buckeye Card arrived!" I told him he didn't have to tell the whole neighborhood how old I was.

So here I am at a high school football game, standing at attention and facing the flag while the home team's band plays the national anthem. Tears start flowing down my cheeks. All I can see is Red's flag-draped casket at the cemetery. Only a few times have I made it through those few minutes without tears.

At the end when I get home, I miss the "Did we win?" that came the moment I opened the door. I can't give an energetic "Yes!" or a noncommittal "Nah."

I still watch football and college basketball games on TV, but I don't have anyone to yell with—or against.

When I was in Myrtle Beach with my support group, we women decided on the spur of the moment to get our nails done. Mine really needed help. Wow! It made me feel great. I go periodically for a manicure, just like I go regularly for a massage.

I'm not doing this to attract anyone. It's something I could have done a long time ago. I just decided I needed it. For some things I do, I think I'm following Red's advice that if the opportunity comes up and I pass on it, I'll kick myself for the rest of my life.

Rarely do I cook. I long for potlucks so I can fix something in the Crock-Pot. For my meals, I'll open a can of soup or get a container of homemade soup out of the freezer. Cheese sandwiches—grilled or not—are a mainstay. Salads are my forte. I have gift cards for restaurants, so I can eat out occasionally. I also have a few single female friends who don't like to eat alone, so we'll go together for dinner in a group.

So often I get mail addressed to "Hugh Latimer or Current Resident" that I've said I'm going to change my name to Current Resident.

I've learned to laugh again, but sometimes I do get lonely, especially at night with no one to share experiences with.

I tell myself almost daily I'm having fun.

I know I'll never get over Red and his decision, but I'll get through it. Meanwhile, the bills keep coming and the grass keeps growing.

Acknowledgments

In the years since my husband took his life, I have learned a lot and gained a lot of support. Thanks to my friends in my local Survivors of Suicide Bereavement Support Group, I was encouraged to write. These people talked about journaling as a way to express grief. Being a writer, I turned the start of one of my journals into this book.

Although I have said very little about the cause of death to some of my closest friends, I did tell them about writing this book. And I thank many of them for commenting that what I am doing will help others.

Thanks also to my fellow SOS members, I slowly became able to speak publicly about what happened and why.

This was a hard story to tell, but it is one I felt was necessary.

If or when you feel you need help, seek it. Professionals are there to help you.

Now if you'll pardon me, I have bills to pay, and the young man a couple of houses down or the man kitty-corner from me will be coming by to mow my yard. I hope you enjoyed my story.

Printed in the United States
By Bookmasters